南無觀自在菩薩

关于作者

我在中国出生,并于上个世纪90年代初移居美国。在纽约市 Baruch College 的 Zicklin School of Business,我取得了金融与投资的学位。毕业后,我在华尔街的一家世界500强企业开始了我的金融职业生涯。目前,我担任美国国际华严会秘书长,并同时也是美国佛教联合会的英文秘书。 自1991年起,我开始了对佛教的探索,并在已故中国临济禅宗第44代传人本焕大和尚（1907-2012）的引导下皈依了佛、法和僧三宝。

  我一直抱有这样的愿望：希望每个读到这部经文的人都能迅速领会其中的核心思想。因此，在完成《金刚经》的通俗英文翻译之后，我决定将其进一步翻译成现代白话文。如各位所见，我尽量采用了日常生活中的用语。佛法浩渺无际，我为能分享我的译著而心怀感激。

序言

《金刚经》全名《金刚般若波罗蜜经》,被誉为佛教中的无上法宝,以若干不同译本和历代不同大师的注释闻名于世。鸠摩罗什大师翻译的《金刚经》是汉译本中广泛传颂的版本,被视为最经典。

《金刚经》是佛陀与弟子须菩提之间在古印度花园里的深入对话。经典从"云何应住,云何降伏其心"而展开,整部经书阐释了佛教的般若智慧,核心理念之一:空性。简而言之,空性意味着所有事物都是因缘和合而成,没有自性。这一理念启发我们对待世界的方式,并教导我们摒弃对事物的执着。在佛教看来,执着是痛苦的根源,因为我们时常对事物产生错误的认知和深深的执着,这导致痛苦和不满的产生。

《金刚经》的重要性在于它教导如何理解和实践空性的智慧。通过理解空性,我们能够看清事物的真实本质，超越执着，解脱烦恼，拥有内心的平和与宁静。对每个普通人来说，这具有深刻的意义，因为它提供了应对生活中的挑战和困难的智慧。借助《金刚经》中的教导，我们可以更好地应对压力、焦虑和生活中的不确定性，拥有更美好的人生、更加自在祥和的生活。

这本《金刚经》的价值不仅体现了佛陀大智慧对众生的启发。它还是一座跨越文化和语言的桥梁，联结我们所有人，提醒我们共同渴望的涅槃彼岸：摆脱痛苦、追求快乐、得大自在。

今黄平平居士怀着一颗慈悲之心，她译著《金刚经现代白话文》，我由衷赞叹她的付出，并希望能有更多的发心人加入这一工作，将佛法的智慧传播到世界的每个角落。正如佛陀教导的那样，慈悲和智慧应该被传递给世界的每一个生命，无论他们的背景和信仰如何。因此，我鼓励每位读者参与"弘法是家务，利生为事业"的这项弘法工作，以让这份智慧之光照耀我们共同的家园。

愿这本中英文《金刚经现代白话文》为您带来智慧和解脱。

释明予
美国佛教联合会会长
2023年10月11日于美国纽约

前言

美国国际华严会的陈绍恭会长珍藏了一本珍贵的书籍——"宋板东坡手写金刚经",这是他的恩师美国寿冶老和尚赠予的珍贵礼物。这本经典是由文学巨匠苏轼亲手书写的,苏轼在诗、文、书法、绘画等领域留下了永恒的印记,同时深受佛学的影响。苏轼不仅通晓佛经,领悟佛法,还将佛学的思想融入了自己的文学创作之中。他的书法技艺位居"宋四家"之首,包括苏轼、黄庭坚、米芾、蔡襄,而从这本《宋板东坡手写金刚经》中可见,苏轼的书法兼具婉约之美和"文章学问之气",富有永恒的内涵。

2021年,陈绍恭会长怀着一份大愿,计划在全球发行100万套《宋板东坡手写金刚经》。作为美国国际华严会的秘书长,我积极支持这一善举,并已与世界各地的大学和图书馆建立联系,将这本珍贵的经典赠送给他们,并提供英文版本。我们期望每个国家至少有一所大学能够珍藏这本《宋板东坡手写金刚经》及其英文翻译。迄今为止,我们已经将这些宝贵的经典捐赠给包括哈佛大学在内的许多高等院校，以及世界各地的佛教寺庙收藏供养。

然而，许多西方人因不懂中文而无法领略金刚经的智慧。《宋板东坡手写金刚经》仅以书法示人，难以传达佛陀的教诲。因此，我决定将金刚经翻译成英文，以便在捐赠《宋板东坡手写金刚经》时，同时附上英文翻译本，使西方人更容易理解和学习金刚经的智慧。

在出版和传播《宋板东坡手写金刚经》的过程中，我们发现许多人因为文言文的障碍而在理解经文时遇到了困难。因此，我将金刚经翻译成白话文，以助更多人理解金刚经的教义。自1991年起，我开始接触佛法，于1994年皈依了佛教泰斗本焕老和尚，法名常安，至今已经有30余年的佛法修行经验。我将个人的理解融入到这个翻译中，以通俗易懂的语言表达金刚经的智慧，与大家共享。

黄平平
2023年10月7日 于是纽约

《金刚经》现代白话文
黄平平 译著

总策划：陈绍恭

美编设计：黄平平

插图：陈绍恭

出版社：国际华严出版社

Email: huayanusa@gmail.com

发行单位：谷歌图书　　布乐伯图书

The International Hua-Yan Publishing House

国 际 华 严 出 版 社　　纽 约

观自在菩萨，行深般若波罗蜜多时，照见五蕴皆空，度一切苦厄。舍利子，色不异空，空不异色，色即是空，空即是色，受想行识，亦复如是。舍利子，是诸法空相，不生不灭，不垢不净，不增不减。是故空中无色，无受想行识，无眼耳鼻舌身意，无色声香味触法，无眼界，乃至无意识界，无无明，亦无无明尽，乃至无老死，亦无老死尽，无苦集灭道，无智亦无得。以无所得故，菩提萨埵，依般若波罗蜜多故，心无挂碍，无挂碍故，无有恐怖，远离颠倒梦想，究竟涅槃。三世诸佛，依般若波罗蜜多故，得阿耨多罗三藐三菩提。故知般若波罗蜜多，是大神咒，是大明咒，是无上咒，是无等等咒，能除一切苦，真实不虚。故说般若波罗蜜多咒，即说咒曰：揭谛揭谛，波罗揭谛，波罗僧揭谛，菩提萨婆诃。

癸卯季春於碧陈绶书

谨将此书献给临济宗第44代传人本焕大和尚，我从他那里皈依了佛、法、僧三宝；献给密显法师，我从他那里得到了空性的深刻教诲；献给我已故的哥哥黄超云，我今生第一次是从他那里知道了这部《金刚经》的存在。

一切有为法

如梦幻泡影

如露亦如电

应作如是观

 Instagram

 Youtube Channel

 facebook page

无上甚深微妙法，百千万劫难遭遇；
我今见闻得受持，愿解如来真实义。

《金刚般若般罗密经》白话文

第一，法会的缘起

如下是我阿难在现场亲耳听到、亲眼见到的。当时，佛陀和一直跟随佛陀的一千二百五十位大比丘僧弟子们都住在舍卫国的祇树给孤独园内。有一天，到了吃午饭的时候，佛陀穿上袈裟，拿起僧人乞食的饭钵，带领着众弟子们走进舍卫城，并按照佛教戒律里的仪轨乞食。他们不分贫富贵贱，用平等慈悲的心挨家挨户地托钵乞食。随后，他们又都回到祇树给孤独园中用餐。吃过午餐后，佛陀将他的僧衣和饭钵收拾好，清洗他的双足，铺好法座，然后便盘上双腿坐在法座上面。

第二，须菩提提问

这时，在阿罗汉中对空性的义理了解最深，被称为解空第一的长老须菩提，从人群中站起来。他偏袒著右肩，右膝着地，双手合掌，虔诚恭敬地对佛陀说："世间希有，伟大的佛陀！您念念不忘教导我们这些修菩萨道的人。而且特别叮嘱我们，要好好的管理和降伏我们这一颗妄想心。请问佛陀，对于那些已经发起无上正等正觉成佛之心的男女修行者，他们该如何管理和降服他们的妄想心呢？"

佛陀回答说："很好，很好，须菩提！正如你所说，佛陀念念不忘教导诸位男女菩萨修行者，并且时时特别叮嘱诸菩萨们。你们现在认真细听，我为你们解说。那些已经发起无上正等正觉成佛之心的男女菩萨们，他们应该像我下面所讲的这样管理和降服他们的妄想心。"

长老须菩提欢喜地说："好的，佛陀！我们大家都非常喜悦地来倾听您的开示。"

第三，大乘佛教

佛陀对须菩提说："各位菩萨，大菩萨们，应当如下面所讲的这样管理和降服他们的妄想心。所有一切众生，无论是哪一类的生命体，无论是卵生、胎生、湿生、化生的生命体；有色身或者无色身的生命体；有念头活动或者无念头活动的生命体；甚至那些有时有念头活动，有时又没有念头活动的生命体，只要他们能按下面所讲的这样来管理和降服他们的妄想心，他们都能进入究竟圆满的无余涅槃境界。"

"值得提醒大家的是，这样的修持方法能救度无量无数无边的众生。这是为什么呢？其实众生也只是假名，并不符合佛教不生不灭真实存在的定义。众生的存在只是因缘和合有条件而生成的，是有生灭变化的，因此不是真实存在的，是虚妄的。在绝对的角度，众生不存在。在相对的角度，众生是相对的存在。"

"佛陀是从绝对圆满的角度看一切事物。因此从绝对的角度，并没有不生不灭真实存在的众生被我所度化。须菩提！如果有菩萨错误地认为有一个不生不灭真实存在的我、人、众生、寿者，并错误地对并不是真实存在的我、人、众生、寿者产生执着，那么这位菩萨就不是一名真正的菩萨。"

第四，不着相

"还有，须菩提，万法都是因缘和合有条件而生成的，没有一个恒常不变的特征，不是真实存在的，其本质是空性的。菩萨对一切法都应该有这样的认知，并且一点都不应当执着。例如，菩萨在修习六波罗蜜法门中的布施波罗蜜时，不可以错误地认为事物的外在形相是真实存在的，更不可以对事物的外在形相产生执着心。用执着事物外在形相的心去布施，不是修布施波罗蜜。同样的道理，菩萨也不可以因为执着于事物的声音、气味、味道、触摸时的感觉和心中的念头，即声香味触法，而去修布施波罗蜜。"

"菩萨在修习布施波罗蜜时，不可以执着有一个布施的我，不可以执着有一个接受布施的对象，也不可以执着被我所布施的物品。为什么这么说呢？因为去布施的我，接受布施的对象和被我所布施的物品，都是因缘和合有条件而生成的，没有一个恒常不变的特征，不是不生不灭的，不是真实存在的，其本质是空性的。执着是苦，更何况去执着一个本不是真实存在的东西，将创造一个未来苦的因。有执着的布施是有相布施，有相布施不是修布施波罗蜜。菩萨要修习没有任何执着的无相布施，无相布施才是修布施波罗蜜。菩萨修习无相布施所招感的福德广大无边。"

"须菩提，你有办法想像东方的虚空实际有多广大吗？"

"佛陀，我没有办法想像东方的虚空实际有多广大。"

"须菩提，你有办法想像南方、西方、北方、东南方、西南方、东北方、西北方以及上方和下方的虚空实际有多广大吗？"

"佛陀，我没有办法想像。"

"须菩提，菩萨用没有任何执着的心来修无相布施波罗蜜时，相应所得到的福德就如同十方虚空一样广大，无量无边，不可思议。因此，菩萨在修习布施波罗蜜时，要修无相布施。"

第五，认识佛的真实身体

"须菩提，当你见到我这个血肉之躯时，你是不是认为你已经看到了佛陀的真身呀？"

"这个血肉之躯是佛陀的化身，是由地、水、火、风四大在因缘条件成熟的时候和合而生成的。佛陀的化身有生灭，有生死，没有一个恒常不变的特征，不是真实存在的，其本质是空性的。而佛陀的真身是佛的法身，法身无相状并且一直是无处不在。这个血肉之躯不是法身，更不是佛的真身。"

佛陀对须菩提说："不仅佛的血肉之躯不是真实存在的，凡是因缘和合有条件而生成的一切，都不是真实存在的；从究竟的角度来讲，都是有生灭的，都是空性的，因此都是虚妄的。如果一位菩萨，能够在看到事物有条件的、相对存在的同时，也能够看到事物不是真实存的、空性的一面，那么我们可以说这位菩萨见到了佛的真身，即法身。"

第六，正信的稀有可贵

须菩提问佛陀："佛陀！未来的众生，当他们听到您如上所讲的教诲后，能对您讲的道理产生真实的信心吗？"

佛陀对须菩提说："你不要生起这样的怀疑心。在我灭度五百年以后，仍会有修持戒律和福德的人出现。他们能够领悟我上面所说的道理，并对这个道理产生真实的信心。你要知道，这些人过去不仅在一位佛、二位佛、三位佛、四位佛或五位佛那里听闻过佛法，多劫以来，他们还在无数位佛那里听闻过佛法并种植善根。当他们再次有机缘听到如上的道理时，只要生起一念的清净信心，须菩提，对此佛陀将完全了解。他们将获得佛陀的加持，将获得无量的福德。为什么这么说呢？这些善根众生通晓我相、人相、众生相和寿者相都不是真实存在的，因此不会执着我相、人相、众生相和寿者相；他们通晓缘起而产生的生灭的法相，不是真实存在的，因此不会执着法相；他们通晓空相的本来面目是没有一个相状，即无相，他们也不会执着空相。"

"只要心中执着一个相状,那么就是执着我相、人相、众生相和寿者相;若执着法相,那么就是执着我相、人相、众生相和寿者相;若执着空相,那么就是执着我相、人相、众生相和寿者相。不可以执着于佛陀所说的正法;也不可以执着那些非佛法的东西。因此,佛陀常说:你们诸位比丘一定要知道,我所说的佛法,就如同那渡人到对岸的船。到达彼岸之后,就应立即弃舟登岸了。没有悟道时,我们需要依佛法来修持。可是悟道后,也不可以对佛法产生执着。我们既要放弃对佛法的执着,更应该放弃对非佛法的执着。"

第七,万法皆空

"须菩提!你是否认为佛陀证得的无上正等正觉,阿耨多罗三藐三菩提法,有一个固有不变的真实存在的体性和相状?你是否认为佛陀说的法有一个固有不变的真实存在的体性和相状?"

须菩提回答说:"就我对佛陀教法的理解,无上正等正觉这个法没有一个固有不变的真实存在的体性和相状，其本质是空性的。佛陀说法随着种种因缘说不同的法，时空不同，讲的内容不同。因此佛陀说的法没有一个固有不变的真实存在的体性和相状，其本质也是空性的。所谓万法皆空，我们不可以执着一切法。我们即不可以执着有，也不可以执着空。正因为这样，我们说一切贤圣的差别，在于他们对无为法、空性理解的深浅程度不同而有差别。"

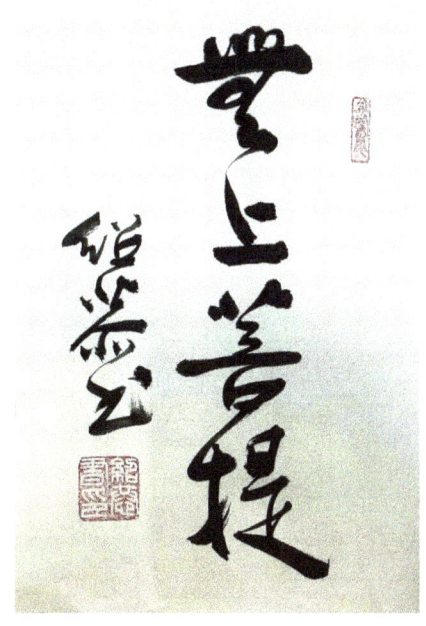

第八，福德

"须菩提，假如有人拿出能装满三千大千世界这么多的七宝布施，这个人所得的福德多不多呢？"须菩提回答："佛陀，非常多。我之所以这么说，是因为这个布施的人了解福德没有一个不变的真实存在的体性和相状，其本质是空性的。所以不会执着因布施而带来的福德。佛陀说这样不执着任何相状的布施所获得的福德多。"

佛陀说："如果有人能正确地理解和遵守奉持这部经或者只有这部经中的四句偈颂，并能够正确地在空性的角度为他人解说，那么，这个人所得的无相福德，比前面布施七宝的人所得的有相福德还要多。"

"为什么这么说呢？须菩提，一切诸佛，以及诸佛所证悟的阿耨多罗三藐三菩提法，都离不开这部经里讲的无相的概念。须菩提，佛法虽有妙用，但是佛法并没有一个不变的真实存在的体性和相状，佛法的本质也是空性的，所谓万法皆空。但是为了沟通的目的，权且安立一个名称，佛法。"

第九，所谓的相不是真实存在

"须菩提！你觉得须陀洹会不会有这样的想法：我已证得须陀洹果，初果阿罗汉，这个须陀洹果是真实存在的。"

须菩提答："不会的，佛陀！为什么呢？须陀洹是初果阿罗汉，也被称为初入圣人之道者或入流者。意思是说他们不会对色尘、声尘、香尘、味尘、触尘和法尘产生执着。须陀洹不会有这样的心念：我已证得须陀洹果。这个须陀洹果是不生不灭真实存在的。"

"须菩提！你觉得斯陀含会不会有这样的心念：我已证得斯陀含果，二果阿罗汉，这个斯陀含果是不生不灭真实存在的。"

须菩提答："不会的，佛陀！为什么呢？斯陀含的意思是说在证得涅槃前，他们只要往天界投胎一次，再回到人间做人一次，他们就可以证得涅槃。所以斯陀含也叫一往来，一次往天上，一次回来人间。

然而，斯陀含的一次往天上，一次回来人间投胎，是有条件而产生的，是空性的，不是不生不灭真实存在的。斯陀含不会有这样的心念：我已证得斯陀含果，这个斯陀含果是不生不灭真实存在的。"

"须菩提！你觉得阿那含会不会有这样的心念：我已证得阿那含果，三果阿罗汉，这个阿那含果是不生不灭真实存在的。"

须菩提答："不会的，佛陀！为什么呢？阿那含的意思是说在证得涅槃前，他们不会再来欲界投胎。然而，在阿那含的心中，那个不回欲界投胎的我和欲界，都是有条件而生的，都是空性的，都不是不生不灭真实存在的。阿那含不会有这样的心念：我已证得阿那含果，这个阿那含果是不生不灭真实存在的。"

"须菩提！你觉得阿罗汉会不会有这样的心念：我已证得阿罗汉，四果阿罗汉，这个阿罗汉果是不生不灭真实存在的。"

须菩提答："不会的，佛陀！为什么呢？阿罗汉之所以被称为阿罗汉，是因为阿罗汉已经证得我空，具备了脱生死，不再在生死中轮回的能力。如果一位阿罗汉认为：'我已经取得了阿罗汉的成就，并且这个成就是不生不灭真实存在的。'那么这个人就是执着我相、人相、众生相和寿者相。阿罗汉不会有这样的心念：我已证得阿罗汉果，这个阿罗汉果是不生不灭真实存在的。"

"佛陀，您说我已证得不执着我相、人相、众生相、寿者相，破除人我对立的无诤三昧，是人中第一，亦为罗汉中的第一离欲阿罗汉。但我知道阿罗汉也是有条件而生的，是空性的。所以我从不执着于我是离欲阿罗汉的想法。佛陀，如果我对阿罗汉的成就有执着，认为这些成就都是真实存在的，佛陀就不会赞歎我是一个喜欢内心进入无诤、真正寂静处的阿兰那行者。我知道阿兰那行也是有条件而生的，是空性的，所以我不去执着有条件而生成的阿兰那行。这样佛陀才说须菩提喜欢阿兰那行。"

第十，净土庄严

佛陀问须菩提："我在过去世是燃灯古佛的学生。他当时是这个世界的佛教教主。你觉得那个时候，我从燃灯佛陀那里，有没有学到过任何不是有条件而生的，是不生不灭真实存在的妙法呢？"

"没有的，佛陀。您当时在向燃灯古佛学习佛法时，您没有得到任何不生不灭真实存在的、无条件而产生的佛法，因为佛法的本质是空性的。所谓万法皆空。但是，在相对的层面，您在燃灯佛那里学习了相对存在的、有功用的佛法，并依相对存在的佛法修行。"

"须菩提，从绝对的角度来看，你觉得菩萨的行为有没有令佛土庄严呢？"

"没有，佛陀。为什么这么说呢？我们说菩萨庄严佛土，这包括菩萨的化身、菩萨付出的努力，以及佛土。但菩萨的化身、菩萨的努力以及佛的净土，都只是有条件而生成的，是空性的，从究竟的角度看并不是不生不灭真实存在。但是为了沟通的目的，权且说菩萨庄严佛土。"

"须菩提，因此所有菩萨和大菩萨都要生起清净心，不要执着色尘，也不要执着声音、气味、味道、触觉和念头。他们应该在生起清净心的同时，不执着于任何东西。"

"须菩提，假设有一个人的身体像须弥山一样巨大，你怎么想？你会觉得这个身体大吗？"

须菩提说："佛陀，那是极其巨大的。但是多么巨大的身体也只是暂时的存在，是有条件而生的。它不是一个不生不灭真实存在的身体，从绝对的角度来看是空性的。为了沟通的目的，佛陀权且说它的身体巨大。而真正的大身是佛陀的法身，法身无相，大到无法用计量单位来测量，法身才是真正的大身。"

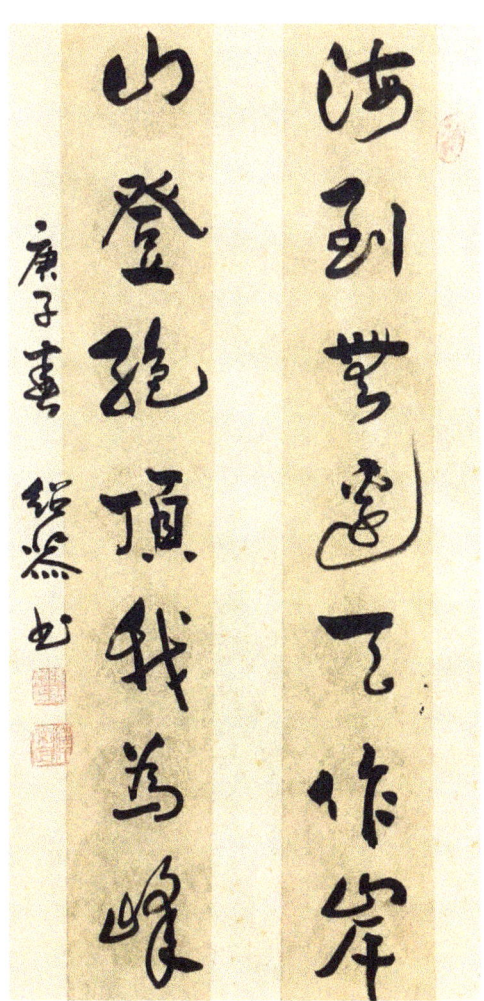

海到無邊天作岸

山登絕頂我為峰

庚子春紹基書

觀自在菩薩行深般若波羅蜜多時，照見五蘊皆空，度一切苦厄。舍利子，色即是空，空即是色，色不異空，空不異色，受想行識亦復如是。舍利子，是諸法空相，不生不滅，不垢不淨，不增不減。

第十一，从无相中生出的福德最大

"须菩提，如果将恒河中的每一粒沙都转化为一条恒河，那么我们将拥有如此众多的恒河，其数量与恒河中的沙粒一样多。如果将这些恒河中的所有沙粒相加，你会不会认为这是一个极其巨大的数字呢？"

须菩提回答道："佛陀，那将是一个极为庞大的数字。如果将每一粒沙变成一条恒河，并将这些恒河相加，其总数已经如此之大，以至于无法计算，更不用说计算所有这些恒河里的沙粒总数了。这个数字之巨大已经超越了我们的想象，数也数不清楚。"

"须菩提，现在假设我们将所有这些恒河中的沙粒数量的总和标记为X，那么，如果有一位男性或女性菩萨修行者能够布施足够多的七宝，使其能够装满X个三千大千世界，你认为这个人所获得的福德多吗？"

须菩提回答说："佛陀，这位男性或女性菩萨修行者因此将获得的福德实在是太多了，多得我们甚至无法相像。"

"须菩提，我要真诚地告诉你，只要一个有德行的人，无论男女，只要能够正确理解和受持这部经，或者其中的四句偈颂，并且能够以空性的角度为他人解说，那么，这个人所获得的无相福德，要比之前布施七宝的人所获得的有相福德多得多。"

第十二，护持正见

"还有须菩提，不论在哪里，一个人只要能正确地理解和遵守奉持这部经或者只有这部经中的四句偈颂，并能够正确地在空性的角度为他人解说，这个说经的地方，一切世间的天人、人、阿修罗等，都应该前来护持、恭敬供养，就如同护持、恭敬供养佛的塔庙一样。如果有人能正确地理解和遵守奉持这部经，这个人将大彻大悟，见性成佛。因此，这部经典所在的地方，就是佛的住处，应当恭敬供养。这位佛弟子也值得我们尊重。"

第十三， 以正确的方式修行

　　须菩提请问佛陀："佛陀，我们应该给这部经典起什么名字呢？我们应该如何按这部经典的教诲修行呢？"

　　佛陀说："就给这部经命名为《金刚般若波罗蜜经》，意为空性的智慧犹如金刚般锋利，不为万物所摧毁，却能摧毁一切万物，能断一切烦恼，把我们从痛苦的此岸带到解脱的彼岸。你们就按照经名的真正含义来修行。为什么这么说呢？须菩提,佛陀讲的这个般若波罗蜜，是在讲空性的智慧。但是般若波罗蜜这个法门是因缘和合有条件而生成，没有一个恒常不变的特征，不是不生不灭真实存在的，其本质是空性的。为了语言沟通的方便，佛陀用般若波罗蜜这个词来告诉我们获得解脱的空性智慧。须菩提， 你认为佛陀有没有教过本质不是空性的法门呢？ "

　　" 没有， 佛陀。"

"须菩提,你觉得把三千大千世界中所有的微尘都加在一起,这个数目大不大呢?"

须菩提回答说:"佛陀,非常大。"

"须菩提,微尘是因缘和合而成,没有一个恒常不变的特征,不是不生不灭真实存在的,其本质是空性的。但是为了语言沟通的方便,便用微尘来代替所讲的物质。三千大千世界也是因缘和合有条件而生成的,没有一个恒常不变的特征,不是不生不灭真实存在的,其本质也是空性的。但是,从相对的角度,为了语言沟通的方便,用三千大千世界来描述一个空间范围。"

"须菩提!你认为是否可以通过一个人身体拥有的三十二个特征来识别佛性呢?"

"佛陀,不可以。理由是佛陀身上的三十二个特征是因缘和合有条件而生成,没有一个恒常不变的特征和体性。佛陀身上的三十二个特征不是不生不灭真实存在的，其本质是空性的。生灭的、有相的佛陀身上的三十二个特征不能和无相的佛性相提并论。"

"须菩提，如果有德行的人，不论男女，用如恒河中沙粒那么多数量的身体和性命来修习布施法门；而另一个人，只要能正确地理解和遵守奉持这部经或者只有这部经中的四句偈颂，并能够正确地在空性的角度为他人解说，这个人所获得的无相福德远远超过前面用身体和性命行布施的人所获得的有相福德。"

第十四，不住相

须菩提听了佛陀对空性实相的教诲后，感动得热泪盈眶，对佛陀说："佛陀，虽然我已证得阿罗汉，但我从来没有听到过如此甚深微妙的智慧。佛陀，如果有人在听完这部经典后，能明心见性，体悟到宇宙人生空性的实相。那么，我们可以判断这个人已经获得了最上第一希有的无相功德。佛陀，宇宙人生的实相就是空相，不可得。为了沟通的目的，佛陀权且用实相这个词汇来表达义理。"

"佛陀，我现在听到这部经典，并能正确地理解和遵守奉持这部经典的真正义理，这并不困难。但是五百年后，如果有人能遇到这部经典，并能正确地理解和遵守奉持这部经典的真正义理，我们要知道，这样的人可真是第一希有、了不起的人啊！"

"为什么这么说呢？因为这个人已经体悟到我相、人相、众生相、寿者相都不是不生不灭真实存在的。这个人已经体悟到我相、人相、众生相、寿者相的本质都是空性的，所以这个人不会执着我相、人相、众生相、寿者相。只要是见到空性，不执着于任何的相，那么这个人便可被称为佛陀。"

佛陀对须菩提说："是的，是的。如果有人听完这部经典深妙的空性义理后，能够不感到震惊、不感到恐惧、不感到害怕，那么这个人是非常难得的。为什么这么说呢？须菩提，那是因为这个人了悟佛陀所说的第一波罗蜜，即空、无相、解脱的智慧。第一波罗蜜，并没有一个恒常不变的，不生不灭真实存在的相状，其本质也是空性的。为了沟通的目的，佛陀权且用第一波罗蜜这个词汇来表达。须菩提，同样的道理，忍辱波罗蜜并没有一个恒常不变的，不生不灭真实存在的相状，本质也是空性的。为了沟通的目的，佛陀权且用忍辱波罗蜜这个词汇来表达。"

"须菩提,在我的过去世,当我的身体被歌利王肢解时,我并没有执着我相、人相、众生相、寿者

相。如果在那个时候，我对我相、人相、众生相、寿者相中的任何一个相有执着，那么我一定会产生憎恨心。但在当时，我没有任何的憎恨心。"

"须菩提，我过去世曾经用了五百世修习忍耐，最后成就忍辱波罗蜜。我能够做到心中无我相、无人相、无众生相、无寿者相。所以说啊，须菩提，菩萨应该在不执着任何相、远离一切相的基础上，发无上正等正觉，成佛的大愿。菩萨不可以在执着色尘的基础上起心动念；菩萨不可以在执着声尘、香尘、味尘、触尘、法尘的基础上起心动念；菩萨应该在不执着任何相状的基础上起心动念。如果菩萨的心执着任何一个相状，那么这位菩萨就会有烦恼，心就不能正确的起心动念，不能正确地安住。"

"所以佛陀常说：为了利益一切众，菩萨不可以因执着色尘以及声尘、香尘、味尘、触尘、法尘而行布施。佛陀说一切的相，其本质是空性的；所有众生，其本质也是空性的。须菩提！佛陀不讲假话，佛陀讲的话与空性的义理相应，佛陀绝对不会欺诳众生并且佛陀讲的话前后一致。须菩提，佛陀所证悟的法无相，是空性的，同时在因缘条件具足时能产生无限的妙用。如果菩萨的心对菩萨自己布施的这个行为执着的话，就象一个人进入黑暗的地方什么都看不见，这位菩萨就见不到事物的本来面目，见不到空性。如果菩萨的心对于菩萨自己布施的这个行为不执着的话，就像一个视力正常的人，在日光下可以看到万事万物，这位菩萨能见到事物的本来面目，见到空性。"

"须菩提！未来一个有德行的人，不论男女，如果能时常读诵这部经典并且能正确地理解和遵守奉持这部经典的真正义理，慢慢地这个人的智慧将会被开启。无所不知，无所不见的佛陀将对此完全知晓，这个人将会成就无量无边无尽的功德。"

第十五，正确奉持金刚经义理的功德

"须菩提，如果一个有德行的人，不论男女，每天分别在清晨、正午和下午，做三次布施，每次都用如恒河的沙粒数量那么多的身体来施舍，如此经过百千万亿劫都没有间断过；但是，如果有另一个人，在听闻这部《金刚经》后能够觉悟到空性的智慧，建立正确的信仰，并且能够依照佛法的教导去实践，那么这个人所积累的无相功德远远超过前者所积累的有相功德。如果这个人不但能正确地理解和遵守奉持这部经典的真正义理，还能经常书写、读诵或向他人解释这部经典，那么这个人所积累的功德将更为巨大"

"须菩提，总之，佛陀为了那些修持大乘的菩萨，为了那些修持明心见性最上乘法的菩萨们而宣说这部经典。因此，这部经典拥有不可思议、无法估量、无边无际的功德。如果有人能够正确地理解和遵守奉持这部经典的真正义理，并且能够广泛地向他人解说，佛陀以佛陀的智慧对此充分了解，那么这个人将获得不可思议、无边无际、无法估量的功德。这位明心见性之人，将来会承担佛陀无上正等正觉的使命，必定会成功。"

"为什么这么说呢?须菩提,如果一个人执着于二乘人的法,就会执着于我见、人见、众生见、寿者见。这个人将无法理解这部经典的义理,更不会学习、读诵,或向他人解说。因此,须菩提,无论在何处,只要有这部《金刚经》在,一切世间的天人、人、阿修罗等都应当将这个地方看成是一座塔庙,以香花恭敬供养,并应该虔诚地围绕着这个地方礼拜。"

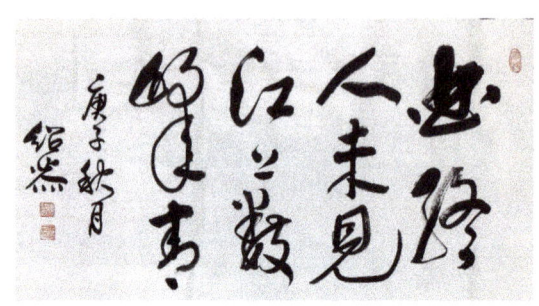

第十六，消累劫业障

"此外，须菩提，一个有德行的人，不管是男还是女，如果这个人能够正确地理解和遵守奉持这部经典的真正义理，并且时常读诵它，但却遭受别人的轻视和诽谤。对于这种情况，你应该明白，这是由于这位修行人过去世的不善业所造成的。通常这样的不善业会导致他们下一世招感去痛苦的三恶道投胎的果报，但是因为他们持诵《金刚经》的缘故，这个人过去世的恶业因为别人的轻视和诽谤而被抵消，这个人将来一定成佛。"

"须菩提，在很久很久以前，在我的过去世，当时的佛是燃灯佛，他是这个世界的导师。我供养了八百四千万亿无量诸佛，没有遗漏过一位佛。然而，如果有人在末法时代，能正确地理解和遵守奉持这部经典的真正义理，并且经常读诵它，那么我所供养诸佛的有相功德抵不上这个人所得的无相功德的百分之一、也抵不上千万亿分之一。这个人所获得的功德极其巨大，大到无法用数字来表达，甚至无法用比喻来正确形容。"

"须菩提，在未来的末法时期，一个有德行的人，不管是男还是女，如果他们能够正确地理解和遵守奉持这部经典的真正义理，并且经常读诵它，所得到的功德将是不可思议，难以置信的。如果我如实地把这些功德都说出来的话，可能会让末法时期的一些人完全不相信，甚至令他们因为极度的不相信而导致心智发狂。须菩提，你要明白，《金刚经》的教义和与之相关的果报都是不可思议的。"

第十七，我即是空

这时，须菩提再次请问佛陀："佛陀，对于那些已经发起无上正等正觉成佛之心的男女修行者，他们该如何管理和降服他们的妄想心呢？"

佛陀回答说："那些已经发起无上正等正觉成佛之心的男女菩萨们，他们应该像我下面所讲的这样发愿：我要救度所有的众生，令他们离苦得乐。然而，我明白众生是五蕴之身，是由五蕴所构成，是因为特定条件的存在才显现的，其本质是空性的。因此，从究竟的角度来看，没有一个众生是不生不灭真实存在的。既然众生并不是真实存在的，因此也不存在需要被救度的众生这回事了。只是为了沟通的方便，我们权且说他们是众生。怎么理解呢？如果一位菩萨认为众生是真实存在的，那么这位菩萨就是执着我相、人相、众生相、寿者相，这位菩萨就不是真正的菩萨。"

"须菩提，一切法都是因缘和合有条件而生成的，它们的本质是空性的，所谓万法皆空。因此，阿耨多罗三藐三菩提，趋向正等正觉的法，并没有一个真实存在的、不变的相状和体性，它同样是空性的。须菩提,你是否认为,当年我向燃灯佛学习佛法的时候,我得到了一个不生不灭的、真实存在的、有一个不变相状和体性的法,叫阿耨多罗三藐三菩提呢?"

"佛陀,就我所理解的佛法,当佛陀向燃灯佛学习佛法的时候,并没有得到一个不生不灭、真实存在、有一个不变相状和体性的法,叫阿耨多罗三藐三菩提。"

"须菩提,你讲得很好,无上正等正觉,阿耨多罗三藐三菩提法的本质是空性的。为了便于沟通,我们权且称之为阿耨多罗三藐三菩提法。如果我当时认为阿耨多罗三藐三菩提法有一个真实存在的相状和体性,燃灯佛就不会为我授记预言:你将在未来世成佛,你成佛时叫释迦牟尼。什么是如来?如来实际上是指那位领悟到一切都如如不动、即空性的人。须菩提,一切法的本质时空性的。因此,佛陀所证悟的无上正等正觉,阿耨多罗三藐三菩提法的本质也是空性的。"

"然而，在相对层面上，无上正等正觉的法则能发挥其作用，并引导佛陀获得了无上正等正觉。因此，我们说无上正等正觉的法既不是在究竟层面上真正存在的，也不是在相对层面上不存在的。在因缘条件都具备的时候，从空性中可以创造出无限的妙有。所谓的一切法都是唯心所造，万法都离不开这一颗心性，离不开清净自性。正因为这样，我们说一切法都是佛法。须菩提，当我们交流时，使用一切法来表达意思，实际上并没有一个不生不灭真实存在东西叫一切法。还是这句话：一切法的本质是空性的，不是真实的存在。比如，我们说一个人的身体又高又大,你认为这个高大的身体是真实存在的吗"

须菩提接着佛陀的话，对佛陀说："佛陀，您说一个人的身体又高又大，那是为了沟通的方便。其实，一个人的身体是因缘和合有条件而生成的，并不是真实的存在，其本质是空性的。同时，即使这个身体再大，也有个尺寸，而真正大的是佛的法身，法身无相，是用尺寸无法度量的。"

"菩萨明白法的本质是空性的道理。一位菩萨如果认为自己度脱的众生是不生不灭的，是真实存在的，那么这位菩萨就没有理解空性的道理，就不是名副其实的菩萨。因此，佛陀说在一切法当中，根本就没有真实存在的我相、人相、众生相和寿者相。这些相根本就不存在。"

"此外，如果一位菩萨看不到空性，认为佛土有一个不生不灭真实存在的相状，那么这位菩萨也不是真正的菩萨。为什么要这么说呢？真正的佛土是我们的清净自性。当我们看到万法的同时，能够体悟到万法当下的空性，令心保持在无所执着的清净状态，这个才是真正的庄严佛土。须菩提，真正的菩萨能够透彻地体悟到我和法都是空性的义理。"

第十八，万法不离一颗真心

佛陀问："须菩提，你认为佛陀有没有肉眼？"

须菩提回答："佛陀有肉眼。"

佛陀问："须菩提，你认为佛陀有没有具备神通力的天眼？"

须菩提回答："佛陀有天眼。"

佛陀问："须菩提，你认为佛陀有没有能够见到一切法的本质是空性的慧眼？"

须菩提回答："佛陀有慧眼。"

佛陀问："须菩提，你认为佛陀有没有能够见一切法的空相，而不对一切法产生的假相执着的法眼？"

须菩提回答："佛陀有法眼。"

佛陀问："须菩提，你认为佛陀有没有能够见到自性的佛眼？"

须菩提回答:"佛陀有佛眼。"

佛陀问:"须菩提,你认为恒河中的沙子多不多?"

须菩提回答:"佛陀,恒河中的沙子很多。"

佛陀问:"须菩提,如果恒河中的每一粒沙都变成一条恒河,把每一条恒河里的沙粒数目都加起来。如果我们把这些沙粒数的总合设定为x。假设有x个佛世界,你认为这么多的佛世界算不算多?"

须菩提回答:"佛陀,太多了。"

佛陀说:"在这么多佛世界里的所有众生的起心动念,佛陀全部知道。为什么这么说呢?那是因为一切众生的心念都是在因缘条件和合时从佛性中产生出来的,而佛性遍一切处。因此,在这么多的佛世界中的所有众生的起心动念,佛陀全部知道。念头没有不生不灭真实存在的体性,在念头产生的同时,就开启了念头生灭的过程，这体现了念头空性的本质。同样的道理，我们说过去心，现在心和未来心都是念头而已，都不是不生不灭真实的存在，本质是空性的。"

第十九，无住相布施福报最大
　　"须菩提，如果有人拿出可以填满三千大千世界那么多的七宝用来布施，你认为这个人因此而得到的福报大不大呢？"

　　"佛陀，这个人因此而得到的福报太大了。"

　　"须菩提，福报的本质是空性的。但是为了沟通的方便，我们权且说得到的福报多。如果一位菩萨了解福报是因缘和合，有条件而产生的真相，了解福报是空性的道理，并且不执着于福报的生灭假相，那么这位菩萨所得到的福报最大。"

第二十，不执着于任何相状而行菩萨道
　　"须菩提，你觉得不生不灭的佛性和化身佛圆满的肉身是不是一回事?"

"佛陀,绝对不是一回事。为什么这么说呢?化身佛圆满的肉身是由地水火风四大组成的,是有条件而产生的,是有生灭的,不是佛性本身。佛性是不生不灭的,是无相的,是佛的真身。为了沟通的目的,佛陀权且用圆满报身这个词汇来表达。"

"须菩提,你觉得不生不灭的佛性,是否可以用化身佛所具有的三十二个相貌特征和八十种好作为标准,来衡量和分辨佛性的真伪呢?"

"佛陀,绝对不可以用化身佛所具有的三十二个相貌特征和八十种好作为标准,来衡量和分辨佛性的真伪。为什么这么说呢?佛性是无相的,而化身佛的三十二个相貌特征和八十种好是因缘和合,有条件而产生的,是有生灭的。因此,三十二个相貌特征和八十种好并不是佛性本身。但是,为了沟通的目的,权且用三十二个相貌特征和八十种好来描述化身佛。"

第二十一，被用语言来表达的东西，并不是真实存在的

"须菩提，绝对不可抱持这样的想法，认为我所说的法都是真实存在的，不生不灭的。为什么这么说呢？如果有一个人说佛陀讲的法是真实存在的，是不生不灭的。那此人根本未能领悟我所讲的法的真实含义和目的。须菩提，万法皆空，我所说的法皆由因缘和合而生起，其本质乃是空性，并没有一样不生不灭、真实存在的东西叫做法。但是，为了便于交流，权且运用'法'这一词汇来表述所传之教义。"

这时，有智慧的须菩提问佛陀："佛陀，未来的众生，当他们听到您现在所讲的关于空性的法，他们能相信和理解您所讲的空性的道理吗？"

佛陀回答说："须菩提，从佛陀究竟的角度来看，没有一个不生不灭真实的、在绝对意义上存在的众生。众生是因缘和合、有条件而生的，因此众生一定会有生灭，不符合佛教真实存在的定义。然而，在凡夫相对的世界中，有相对存在的众生。为了沟通的

目的,我们权且使用众生这个词来描述众生这种相对存在的现象。"

第二十二,无上正等正觉法的本质是空性的

　　须菩提对佛说:"佛陀,您证得被称为无上正等正觉阿耨多罗三藐三菩提法。话虽这么说,但是,佛陀并没有得到一样不生不灭、真实存在的东西,叫做无上正等正觉阿耨多罗三藐三菩提法。"

　　佛陀回答说:"须菩提,你讲得对。佛陀已经证得无上正等正觉阿耨多罗三藐三菩提法,因此,了知一切的法。但是,佛陀并没有得到一样不生不灭、真实存在的东西叫无上正等正觉阿耨多罗三藐三菩提法。阿耨多罗三藐三菩提法是因缘和合有条件而生成的,其本质是空性的,没有一个不生不灭真实存在的相状。但是,为了沟通的目的,权且用阿耨多罗三藐三菩提法这个词来描述这个令众生能够成佛的法。"

第二十三，以不著相的清净心而修一切善法

"还有，须菩提，法都是因缘和合有条件而生成的，所有的法都不拥有一个不生不灭、真实存在的相状。因为一切法都是空性的，所以从空性的角度来看，一切法都是平等的，没有高低之分。如果一位修行人，能够在了知我、人、众生和寿者的本质是空性的基础上修习一切善法，能够在不执着于我、人、众生和寿者的基础上修习一切善法，这位修行人就能够证得阿耨多罗三藐三菩提，无上正等正觉。须菩提，善法也是因缘和合有条件而生成，没有一个不生不灭、真实存在的相状，其本质是空性的。但是，为了沟通的目的，权且用善法这个词来描述。"

第二十四，有相和无相修行所带来的福德无法相提并论

"须菩提，如果三千大千世界中所有的须弥山都是用七宝堆积而成，假如有一个人以执着相状的心态用如此多的七宝施舍。假如有另外一个人，这个人

能够以不执着相状、无相的心受持读诵这本金刚经或者只是受持读诵这本金刚经中的四句偈颂，并且为别人解说其中的义理。那么前者执着相状布施七宝所得的福德远远不及后者不执着相状、无相修行的福德。前者布施七宝所得的福德比不上后者无相修行所得的福德的百分之一；比不上后者无相修行福德的百千万亿分之一。和后者相比，前者所得的福德实在太少，以至于无法用数字清晰地比较两者之间的差距。"

第二十五，众生不是真实存在，本质是空性

"须菩提，你千万不要认为佛陀度脱的众生是真实存在的。众生没有一个不生不灭、真实存在的相状，其本质是空性的。如果佛陀认为众生是真实存在的，那么佛陀就对我、人、众生、寿者有执着。同理，须菩提，佛陀口中说的我，没有一个不生不灭、真实存在的相状，其本质是空性的。遗憾的是，凡夫认为这个血肉之身的我是真实存在的。凡夫没有一个不生不灭、真实存在的相状，其本质也是空性的。为了交流的目的，权且用凡夫这个词表达意思。"

第二十六，法身无相

"须菩提，化身佛有庄严的三十二相，你觉得见到拥有三十二相的化身佛，你就见到真正的佛了吗？"

须菩提回答说："是的，见到拥有三十二相的化身佛，就是见到了真正的佛。"

"须菩提，如果以三十二相作为标准，转轮圣王也拥有三十二相，转轮圣王岂不也是真正的佛了吗？"

须菩提立刻对佛陀说："佛陀，我现在明白了，真正的佛是佛性，是我们的清净本性，佛性是无相的。因此，不能用三十二相作为辨别真正的佛的标准。"

听到这一点,佛陀说了四句偈颂:"如果有人认为能够见到的那个色身是佛的真身--佛性,如果有人认为通过声音可以求得见到佛的真身——佛性;这个人是以有相的心来追求无相的佛性,我们的清净自性。这样的行为是邪道,永远无法见到真正的佛身,也就是见不到我们的清净自性。"

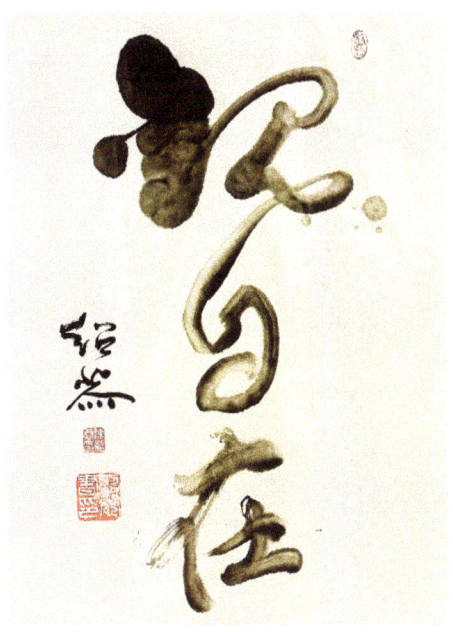

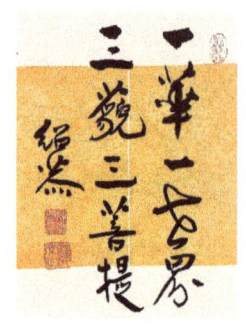

第二十七，不执着法的空相

"须菩提，你如果这样想：既然真正的佛是佛性，而佛性无相。那么化身佛不一定要有三十二相，也同样证得阿耨多罗三藐三菩提，无上正等正觉。须菩提，你千万不要有这样否定因果缘起断灭的想法。为什么呢？我们在发成佛心的同时，不可以执着法的空相，同时也不可以否定因果的相对存在。"

第二十八，不执着于相

"须菩提，如果用七宝填满有如恒河沙那么多的世界的空间，如果有一位菩萨用这么多的七宝做有相的布施；如果有另外一位菩萨能够了知一切法无我，证得空性，那么后者所证得的功德，远远超过前面有相布施所得到的功德。须菩提，原因是后面这些菩萨都不执着福德相。"

须菩提问佛："是什么原因导致这些菩萨都不执着福德相？"

"须菩提，这些菩萨了知所获得的福德，是因缘和合有条件而生成的，没有一个不生不灭、真实存在的相状，其本质都是是空性的。既然菩萨了知福德的本质是空性的，那么菩萨就不会对本不是真实存在的福德产生执着了。"

第二十九，不来不去是如来

"须菩提，如果有人因为看到化身佛行住坐卧，就以为真正的佛身也一定有来、去、坐、卧等相状，并且把这些看成是真实的存在。其实这个人的想法是大错特错了。为什么这么说呢？如来是指佛的清净自性即佛性。佛性的特征是无相。佛性一直都在那里，既没有过来这回事，也没有离去这回事。因为这个特征，我们也称呼佛陀为如来。意思是说佛性一直都在那里，都是那个样子的，没有变化，即所谓的如。"

第三十， 空性无相

"须菩提，如果我们把一个三千大千世界碾碎成一个个的微尘，你说被碾成的微尘粒多不多？"

须菩提回答说："佛陀，太多了。这么多的微尘都没有一个不变的自性，都没有一个不变的相状，是因缘和合有条件而生成的，因此，并不是佛教意义上真实地存在，其本质是空性的。为了交流的目的，权且用微尘这个词表达意思。同理，三千大千世界没有一个不变的自性，没有一个不变的相状，是因缘和合有条件而生成的，也不是佛教意义上真实地存在，其本质是空性的。为了交流的目的，权且用三千大千世界这个词表达意思。"

"三千大千世界是因缘和合有条件而生成，本质是空性的，但是空性本身也没有一个固定的体性和相状存在，空性是无相的。为了交流的目的，权且用一合相来表达缘起法的另外一面，空性。缘起法和空性是任何事物同时存在的两个方面。"

"须菩提，空性只能自己体会，自己感知自己的冷暖。语言文字无法真正表达空性本身。然而，世俗之人错误地认为空性具有一个固定的相状，并执着于这虚幻的相状。"

第三十一，知见的本质是空性的

"须菩提，如果有人说：佛陀总是提到我见、人见、众生见、寿者见，那么我见、人见、众生见、寿者见一定是佛教意义上的真实存在。须菩提，你觉得这个人是不是真正地理解我所表达的真实含义？"

"佛陀，这个人根本不理解佛陀要表达的真实含义。我之所以这么说，那是因为佛陀是为了交流的目的，权且用我见、人见、众生见、寿者见这些词汇来表达。而事实上，我见、人见、众生见、寿者见也都是因缘和合而生成的，其本质是空性的。"

"须菩提，同样的道理，发阿耨多罗三藐三菩提、无上正等正觉成佛之心的修行者，要站在万法本空的角度来看待一切现象，修一切善法。既不执着有，也不执着空。须菩提，佛陀说空相，也是为了交流的目的，权且用空相这个词来表达。你千万别错误地认为空相有一个不变的、真实存在的体性和相状。如果你这样认为，那就是大错特错了。"

第三十二，化身佛不是佛的真身

"须菩提，如果有人用七宝填满无数无量无边的世界，并用这么多数量的七宝修布施。如果另外有修行的男女，能够正确地理解和遵守奉持这部经典或者这部经中四句偈颂里的真正义理，常读诵这部经典，并能广泛地为其他人解说，这后者因此而获得的福德远远大于前面那位用七宝布施的人所获得的福德。为什么呢？那是因为后者能够见到空相，不执着于一切相。"

"一切因缘和合而生成的，都有生灭，都不是佛教意义上的真实存在。它们的出现就像梦境、早晨的露水、天上的雷电，瞬息即逝。我们要以这样的觉知来看待一切现象啊！"

在座的长老须菩提，听完佛陀讲授金刚经之后，连同在场的比丘、比丘尼、优婆塞、优婆夷，以及一切世间的天、人、阿修罗等，都感到充满法喜，并发愿一定要依照佛的教诲理解和实践。

回向偈

愿以此功德，庄严佛净土；
上报四重恩，下济三途苦。
若有见闻者，悉发菩提心；
尽此一报身，同生极乐国。

The Diamond Sutra

Translated by Huang Pingping

 facebook page

 Youtube Channel

 Instagram

Project Director: Chen Shaogong
Graphic Design: Pingping Huang
Paintings by Chen Shaogong
Publisher: The International Hua-Yan Publishing House
Email: huayanusa@gmail.com
Distributed by: Google Books and Blurb Book

The International Hua-Yan Publishing House
国 际 华 严 出 版 社　纽 约

Foreword

The "Diamond Sutra," also known as the "Vajracchedikā Prajñāpāramitā Sūtra," is revered as the ultimate treasure of Buddhism. It has gained worldwide renown for its various translations and commentaries by eminent masters throughout history. Among these, the translation by Master Kumarajiva is widely regarded as the most classical rendition.

The Diamond Sutra" is a profound Buddhist scripture that captures an in-depth dialogue between Buddha and his disciple Subhuti in an ancient Indian garden. The scripture unfolds with the question, "How should a bodhisattva abide, and how should he subdue his mind?" and delves into one of Buddhism's core teachings: emptiness. In essence, emptiness signifies that all phenomena arise from interdependent causes and conditions, devoid of inherent self-nature. This concept inspires us in how we perceive and relate to the world, guiding us to let go of attachments. Buddhism asserts that attachment is the root of suffering, as our misconceptions and strong attachments to things often lead to dissatisfaction and pain.

The significance of the "Diamond Sutra" lies in its teachings on understanding and practicing the wisdom of emptiness. By comprehending emptiness, we can perceive the true nature of things, transcend attachments, and attain inner peace and serenity. This holds profound meaning for every ordinary person, as it provides wisdom to navigate life's challenges and difficulties. Through the teachings of the "Diamond Sutra," we can better cope with stress, anxiety, and life's uncertainties, leading to a more fulfilling and tranquil life.

The value of this "Diamond Sutra" extends beyond the profound wisdom it imparts from the Buddha to all sentient beings. It serves as a bridge that transcends cultures and languages, connecting all of us and reminding us of the common aspiration for Nirvana: liberation from suffering, pursuit of happiness, and attaining great freedom.

Layperson Ms. Pingping Huang, with a heart brimming with compassion, I wholeheartedly applaud her dedication in translating the "Diamond Sutra" into modern Chinese and Englsih. I earnestly hope that more individuals with a compassionate spirit will join this endeavor to disseminate the wisdom of Buddhism to every corner of the world.

Just as the Buddha taught, compassion and wisdom should be shared with every being in the world, regardless of their background and beliefs. Therefore, I encourage every reader to participate in what we often say, "Promoting the Dharma as our responsibility and helping sentient beings as our mission," so that the light of this wisdom may illuminate our common home, the Earth.

May this bilingual Chinese-English "Diamond Sutra" bring you wisdom and liberation.

Mingyu Shi
Chairman, The American Buddhist Confederation
October 11, 2023, in New York, USA

Preface

Mr. Chen Shaogong, president of the International Huayan Buddhist Federation based in New York City, USA, treasures a precious book - "Song Dynasty Edition of Diamond Sutra Handwritten by Su Dongpo." This classic was a cherished gift from his venerable mentor, the old monk Shouye from the United States. The scripture was penned by the literary giant Su Shi (also known as Su Dongpo), who left an indelible mark in fields like poetry, prose, calligraphy, and painting, and was profoundly influenced by Buddhism. Su Shi was not only well-versed in Buddhist scriptures and understood its teachings, but he also integrated Buddhist philosophies into his literary creations. His calligraphic prowess is ranked foremost among the "Four Masters of the Song Dynasty", which include Su Shi, Huang Tingjian, Mi Fu, and Cai Xiang. Through this "Song Dynasty Edition of Diamond Sutra Handwritten by Su Dongpo", one can perceive that Su Shi's calligraphy embodies both a graceful beauty and the "the scholarly tone of the composition," exuding timeless profundity.

In 2021, President Chen Shaogong, with a grand aspiration, planned to distribute 1 million sets of the "Song Dynasty Edition of Diamond Sutra Handwritten by Su Dongpo" worldwide. As the Secretary-General of the International Huayan Buddhist Federation, I wholeheartedly supported this noble initiative. I have actively established connections with universities and libraries around the world, gifting them this invaluable scripture and providing its English version. We hope that at least one university in every country will treasure both the "Song Dynasty Edition of Diamond Sutra Handwritten by Su Dongpo" and its English translation. To date, we have gifted these cherished scriptures to many prestigious institutions, including Harvard University, and have ensured they are housed and revered in Buddhist temples worldwide.

However, many in the West, unfamiliar with the Chinese language, find it challenging to appreciate the wisdom of the Diamond Sutra. The "Song Dynasty Edition of Diamond Sutra Handwritten by Su Dongpo" showcases calligraphy but doesn't effectively convey the teachings of the Buddha. Consequently, I decided to translate the

Diamond Sutra into English. This way, when giving the "Song Dynasty Edition of Diamond Sutra Handwritten by Su Dongpo," an English translation is included, making it easier for Western audiences to understand and learn from the wisdom of the Diamond Sutra.

During the publication and distribution of the "Song Dynasty Edition of Diamond Sutra Handwritten by Su Dongpo", we discovered that many encountered difficulties in understanding the scripture due to the barrier of Classical Chinese. As a result, I translated the Diamond Sutra into modern vernacular Chinese, aiding many more in grasping its teachings. I first encountered Buddhism in 1991 and, by 1994, had taken refuge under the renowned Buddhist master and the 44th lineage holder of the Linji school, Ven. Ben Huan, adopting the Dharma name "Chang An". With over 30 years of experience in Buddhist practice, I've infused my personal understanding into this translation. Through clear and accessible language, I've articulated the wisdom of the Diamond Sutra, eager to share it with all.

Pingping Huang

October 7, 2023, in New York City.

I humbly dedicate this book to Ven. Benhuan, the 44th-generation heir of the Linji school, from whom I took refuge in the Triple Gem of Buddha, Dharma, and Sangha. I also dedicate it to Master Mìxiǎn, from whom I received profound teachings on emptiness. Lastly, I dedicate it to my late brother, Huang Chaoyun, through whom I first learned of the existence of the "Diamond Sutra" in this lifetime.

The unsurpassed, profound, and subtle Dharma is rarely met with, even in thousands of millions of eons. I now see, hear, and uphold it. May I understand the true meaning of the Tathagata.

1. The Reason for Teaching This Dharma

What I'm about to share is what I, Ananda, personally heard and witnessed. Once, the Buddha was staying in the Jetavana Monastery in Shravasti with a community of 1,250 great fully ordained venerable monks and devoted disciples. When it was time to eat, the Buddha, along with his disciples, clothed himself in his robe, held his alms bowl, and entered the city to beg for food door to door, following the Buddhist discipline. After he had returned and eaten, the Buddha put away his bowl and robe, washed his feet, arranged his seat, and then sat down.

2. Subhuti's Question

At that moment, the elder and senior monk, Venerable Subhuti, rose from his seat in the assembly. He uncovered his right shoulder, knelt on his right knee on the ground, joined his palms together respectfully, and then asked the Buddha, "Rare World-Honored One! The Buddha has taken good care of all the Bodhisattvas and has instructed them well. When a virtuous man or woman wants to develop the Buddha's mind of anuttara-samyak-sambodhi, has given rise to help all sentient beings attain

Buddhahood, and has given rise to the perfect bodhichitta, how should their minds remain? How should they tame their grasping minds?"

The Buddha replied, "Excellent, excellent, Subhuti! As you have stated, the Buddha has taken good care of all the Bodhisattvas and has instructed them well. Now, listen attentively as I will explain how a virtuous man or woman, who wants to develop the Buddha's mind of anuttara-samyak-sambodhi and has given rise to the perfect bodhichitta, should abide and subdue the mind."

Subhuti responded, "Indeed, World-Honored One, we eagerly listen with joy."

3. Mahayana Buddhism

Buddha said to Subhuti, "Bodhisattvas, great bodhisattvas, should manage and subdue their delusional minds as follows. All sentient beings, regardless of the type of life form they are – whether born from eggs, born from wombs, born from moisture, or spontaneous transformation; whether they possess a physical form or are formless; whether they engage in mental activities or are devoid of mental activities; even those who sometimes have mental activities and at other times do not, as long as they can manage and subdue their delusional minds as described below, I will literate them completely without leaving a single one behind."

"It's worth reminding everyone that such a practice method can save countless sentient beings without limits. Why is this the case? In truth, sentient beings are mere names and do not conform to the Buddhist definition of true existence that transcends birth and death. The existence of sentient beings arises from conditional causes and conditions, and it is subject to birth, death, and change; therefore, it is not a true and inherent existence but rather illusory. From an absolute perspective, sentient beings do not exist. From a relative perspective, the existence of sentient beings is relative."

"Buddha views all things from the perspective of absolute perfection. From this absolute level, there are no truly existing sentient beings who are beyond birth and death that I liberate. Subhuti, if a bodhisattva erroneously believes in the existence of a truly existing self, person, sentient being, or life span that is beyond birth and death and wrongly becomes attached to them when they are not truly existent, then this bodhisattva is not a genuine bodhisattva."

4. Non-attachment to Characteristics

"Furthermore, Subhuti, all phenomena arise from conditions and are devoid of inherent characteristics. They are not truly existent and are essentially empty. Bodhisattvas should have this understanding and should not grasp onto anything. For example, when Bodhisattvas practice the perfection of generosity within the six paramitas, they should not mistakenly think that external appearances of things are inherently real, nor should they develop attachment to the external forms of things. Giving with attachment to the external forms is not the practice of the perfection of giving. Similarly, Bodhisattvas should not become attached to the sounds, smells, tastes, sensations of touch, or thoughts associated with things, in their practice of giving."

"When Bodhisattvas practice the perfection of giving, they should not be attached to the idea of a giver, a receiver, or the items given. Why is that? Because the giver, the receiver, and the items given all arise from conditions and are devoid of inherent characteristics. They are not permanent or truly existent; their essence is emptiness. Attachment is suffering, and even more so when attached to something that is inherently unreal, creating the cause for future suffering. Giving with attachment is not the practice of the perfection of the paramita of generosity. Bodhisattvas should practice generosity without attachment to any particular characteristic. Why is this? If Bodhisattvas practice generosity without attaching themselves to any characteristic, they will accumulate inconceivable merit."

"Subhuti, can you imagine how vast the empty space in the East is?"

"Buddha, I cannot imagine the vastness of empty space in the East."

"Subhuti, can you imagine how vast the empty space in the South, West, North, Southeast, Southwest, Northeast, Northwest, above, and below is?"

"Buddha, I cannot imagine."

"Subhuti, when Bodhisattvas practice the generosity of giving with a mind free from attachment, the merit they receive is as vast, limitless, and inconceivable as the empty space in the ten directions. Therefore, Bodhisattvas should practice giving without any attachment."

5. Recognizing the True Body of the Buddha
"Subhuti, when you see this flesh and blood form of mine, do you think you have seen the true body of the Buddha?

"This flesh and blood form is the Buddha's manifested body, arising from the coming together of the four elements – earth, water, fire, and wind – when the conditions are ripe. The Buddha's manifested body has birth and death, lacks any permanent unchanging characteristic, is not inherently real, and is essentially empty in nature. The true body of the Buddha is the Buddha's Dharma body (dharmakāya), which is the enlightened mind of the Buddha, characterized by formlessness and ever-present ubiquity."

"This flesh and blood form is neither the Dharma body nor the true body of the Buddha."

The Buddha said to Subhuti, "Not only is this flesh and blood form of the Buddha not inherently real, but everything that arises from causes and conditions, too, is not inherently real. From the ultimate perspective, all phenomena undergo birth and death, possess emptiness, and are thus illusory. If a bodhisattva can perceive the conditioned and relative existence of phenomena while also recognizing their lack of inherent reality and their emptiness, we can say that this bodhisattva has glimpsed the true body of the Buddha, namely the Dharma body (dharmakāya)."

6. True Faith Is Rare and Precious

Subhuti said to the Buddha, "The Rare World-Honored One, when people in the future hear the content of this teaching, will they generate true faith?"

The Buddha replied to Subhuti, saying, "Do not harbor such doubts. Even five hundred years after my passing, there will still be individuals who uphold the precepts and cultivate virtues. They will comprehend the truths I have spoken and genuinely have faith in these teachings. You should know that these individuals have not only heard the Dharma from one, two, three, four, or five Buddhas but, over countless eons, have heard the Dharma from innumerable Buddhas and sowed the seeds of goodness. When, once again, they have the opportunity to hear these same truths, as long as they generate a single thought of pure faith, Subhuti, the Buddha fully understands this. They will receive the Buddha's blessings and amass immeasurable merit."

"Why is this so? These virtuous beings comprehend that the characteristics of a self, a person, a sentient being, or the lifespan of a sentient being, are not inherently real; therefore, they refrain from clinging to these characteristics. They understand that all phenomena arising from dependent origination are not inherently real, thus they do not grasp onto these characteristics. They understand that the true nature of emptiness is devoid of any characteristics, it is formless, and they do not grasp onto emptiness."

"As long as one clings to any characteristic or anything, whether it be the characteristic of a self, a person, a sentient being, or the lifespan of a sentient being or even the law of phenomena or emptiness, it will lead to attachment. One should not cling to the teachings of the Buddha, nor should one cling to non-Buddhist phenomena."

"Therefore, the Buddha often says: You, monks, must be aware that the Dharma I have spoken is like a boat for ferrying people across. Once you have reached the other shore, you should promptly abandon the boat and disembark. When you have not yet attained enlightenment, you need to practice in accordance with the Buddha's teachings. However, after enlightenment, you must not cling to the Buddha's teachings. You should not only relinquish attachment to the Buddha's teachings but also let go of attachment to non-Buddha teachings."

7. All Phenomena Are Empty

"Subhuti, do you think that the Buddha has realized the unsurpassed, perfect enlightenment, the teaching of the Anuttara-samyak-sambodhi, with an inherent, unchanging true nature and characteristics? Do you think that the Dharma expounded by the Buddha has an inherent, unchanging true nature and characteristics?"

Subhuti replied, "In my understanding of the Buddha's teachings, the Dharma of unsurpassed, perfect enlightenment does not possess an inherent, unchanging true nature and characteristics; its essence is emptiness. The Buddha expounds the Dharma in accordance with various conditions, varying in time and space, and the content varies accordingly. Therefore, the Dharma taught by the Buddha does not have an inherent, unchanging true nature and characteristics; its essence is also emptiness. It is said that all phenomena are empty, and we should not cling to any phenomena. We should not cling to existence nor cling to emptiness. It is precisely because of this that we speak of distinctions among all the noble ones, based on their varying depths of understanding of the unconditioned and emptiness."

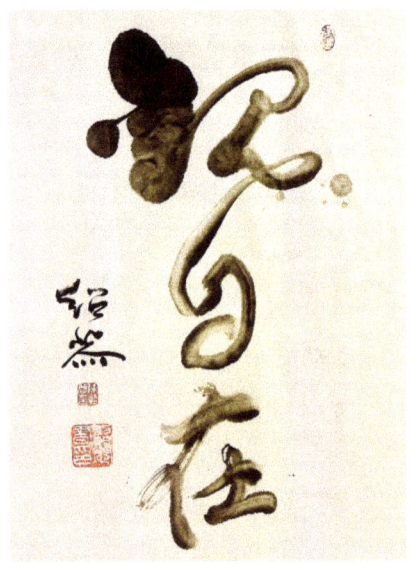

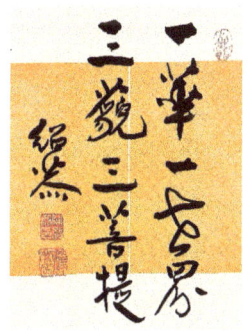

8. Merit

"Subhuti, if someone were to give alms with treasures enough to fill three thousand great thousandfold worlds, would the merit they gain be much or little?"

Subhuti replied, "Buddha, it would be extremely great. I say this because the person giving alms understands that merit does not possess an unchanging, inherently real nature or characteristic; its essence is emptiness. Therefore, they do not cling to the merit brought about by giving. The Buddha teaches that the merit obtained from such giving, free from attachment to any particular aspect, is abundant."

The Buddha said, "If someone can correctly understand and uphold this sutra or even just the four-line verses from it, and can expound it correctly from the perspective of emptiness to others, then the formless merit they attain surpasses the merit of the person who gave the treasures earlier. Why is this so? Subhuti, all Buddhas, along with the supreme, perfect enlightenment they have realized, are inseparable from the concept expounded in this sutra that lacks inherent characteristics. Subhuti, while the Dharma has wonderful applications, it does not possess an unchanging, inherently real nature or characteristics; its essence is emptiness, the so-called 'all phenomena are empty.' Nevertheless, for the sake of communication, a name is provisionally established: the Dharma."

9. The So-Called Forms Are Not Truly Existing

"Subhuti, do you believe a sotapanna thinks they have obtained the accomplishments of a sotapanna and believes that this sotapanna accomplishment truly exists?"

Subhuti said, "No, World-Honored One. Why is that? Sotapanna is named for entering the first level of arahathood and is also called a saintly beginner or a stream-enterer. However, the true essence of sotapanna implies that they will not become attached to any visual object, sound, smell, taste, touch, or mental object. A sotapanna does not think that they have attained the accomplishments of a sotapanna and does not believes that these sotapanna accomplishments are inherently existent."

"Subhuti, do you believe a sakadagami thinks they have obtained the accomplishments of a sakadagami, which is the second level of arahathood, and believes that this accomplishment of the second level of arahathood truly exists?"

Subhuti replied, "No, World-Honored One. Why is that? Sakadagami means that before attaining Nirvana, they need only one more rebirth in a heavenly realm and one more human rebirth. Therefore, they are also called 'one-more-time returner,' signifying one more trip to the heavenly realm and one more return to the human world. However, this one-time journey to the heavenly realm and one-time return to human rebirth are conditional and dependent, thus characterized by emptiness and not truly existing, having no birth and no death. A sakadagami does not think that they have attained the accomplishments of an sakadagami and believes that these sakadagami accomplishments are inherently existent."

"Subhuti, do you believe an anagami thinks they have obtained the accomplishments of a anagamii, which is the third level of arahathood, and believes that this accomplishment of the third level of arahathood truly exists?"

Subhuti replied, "No, World-Honored One. Why is that? Anagami means that before attaining Nirvana, they will not be reborn in the desire realm anymore. However, in the mind of an anagami, both the 'I' that no longer returns to the desire realm and the desire realm itself are conditionally arising, characterized by emptiness, and not inherently existent with no birth and no death. An anagami does not think that they have attained the accomplishments of an anagami and believes that these anagami accomplishments are inherently existent."

"Subhuti, do you believe an arhat thinks they have obtained the accomplishments of an arhat which is the fourth level of arahathood, and believes that this accomplishment of the fourth level of arahathood truly exists?"

Subhuti replied, "No, World-Honored One. Why is that? Arhats are called arhats because they have realized the emptiness of the self and possess the ability to escape birth and death. They are no longer subject to the cycle of samsara. If an arhat were to think, 'I have attained the state of arhatship, and this achievement inherently exists with no birth and no death,' then that person would be attached to the characteristics of a self, a person, a sentient being, and the lifespan. An arhat does not think that they have attained the accomplishments of an arhat and believes that these arhat accomplishments are inherently existent."

"Buddha, you have said that I have attained the non-contention Samadhi, free from attachment to the characteristics of self, person, sentient being, and lifespan of sentient being and that I have broken through the dualism of self and others. You have called me the foremost among humans and the first among arhats in terms of detachment. However, I understand that even arhatship is conditionally arisen and empty in nature. So I do not cling to the idea that I am an arhat who has overcome desires. Buddha, if I were attached to the achievements of an arhat, believing that these accomplishments are inherently real, then you would not praise me as a practitioner of the Araṇa practice who delights in entering the realm of non-abiding and true tranquility within. I understand that even the Araṇa practice arises conditionally and is empty in nature. Therefore, I do not cling to the conditioned arising of the Araṇa practice. It is in this way that you, Buddha, have praised me as one who delights in the Araṇa practice."

10. Majestic Pure Land

The Buddha asked Subhuti, "In a past life, I was a student of the ancient Buddha Dipankara , who was the spiritual leader of this world at the time. Do you think that during that period, I learned any wondrous teachings from Buddha Dipankara that were not subject to conditional existence, that were truly existent, and not subject to birth and death?"

"No, World-Honored One. When you were learning the Dharma from Buddha Dipankara, you did not receive any teaching that were inherently existent, not subject to birth and death, and without conditions because the nature of the Dharma is emptiness, as in the teaching of 'All phenomena are empty.' However, on a relative level, you learned functional teachings from Buddha Dipankara, which have relative existence, and you practiced accordingly based on those relative teachings."

"Subhuti, from an absolute perspective, do you think the actions of a bodhisattva contribute to the adornment of the Pure Land?"

"No, Buddha. Why do I say this? We talk about bodhisattvas adorning the Pure Land, which includes the bodhisattvas' manifestations, their efforts, and the Pure Land itself. However, these manifestations, efforts, and even the Pure Land are all conditionally arisen and possess emptiness, and from an ultimate perspective, they are not inherently existent without birth and death. But for the sake of communication, we can say that bodhisattvas adorn the Pure Land."

"Subhuti, therefore, all bodhisattvas, both ordinary and great, should cultivate pure minds. They should not be attached to forms, nor should they be attached to sounds, smells, tastes, touches, or thoughts. While cultivating pure minds, they should also refrain from attachment to anything."

"Subhuti, suppose there was a person with a body as immense as Mount Sumeru, what do you think? Would you consider this body to be large?"

Subhuti replied, "Buddha, it is indeed immensely vast. However, no matter how vast this body may be, it is still a temporary existence, conditional, and not inherently existing. It is not a truly existing body with neither birth nor death. From an absolute perspective, it is empty in nature. For the purpose of communication, Buddha, you may describe it as having a vast body. The truly great body is Buddha's Dharma body (Dharmakaya), which is formless and immeasurable by any standard of measurement. The Dharma body (Dharmakaya) is indeed the true greatness."

11. The Greatest Merit Arises from Not Clinging to Any Characteristic

"Subhuti, if every grain of sand in the Ganges River were

transformed into another Ganges River, we would have as many Ganges Rivers as there are grains of sand in the Ganges. If we were to add up all these Ganges Rivers, would you think it's an extremely vast number?"

Subhuti replied, "Rare World-Honored One, that would indeed be an immensely vast number. If each grain of sand in the Ganges were transformed into a Ganges River, the sum of these Ganges Rivers would already be so vast that it's incalculable, let alone counting the total number of sand grains within all these Ganges Rivers. This number is beyond imagination and cannot be quantified by mathematics."

"Subhuti, now let's assume we designate the sum of all these sand grains in all the Ganges Rivers as 'X.' If a male or female bodhisattva practitioner were to generously offer enough Seven Treasures to fill X number of the three thousand great thousandfold worlds, would you consider the merit acquired by this person to be substantial?"

Subhuti replied, "Rare World-Honored One, the merit acquired by this male or female bodhisattva practitioner through such an act would be so immense that it's beyond imagination."

"Subhuti, I sincerely tell you that as long as a virtuous person, regardless of gender, correctly understands and upholds this sutra or the four lines of verse within it, and is capable of explaining it to others from the perspective of emptiness, the inconceivable merit acquired by this person, in the form of the formless merit, would far exceed that of the person who gave Seven Treasures."

12. Upholding Right View

"Furthermore, Subhuti, regardless of wherever it may be, as long as a person can correctly understand and uphold this sutra or even just the four-line verses within it, and can explain it to others from the perspective of emptiness, at that place of teaching, all beings, whether heavenly beings, human beings, or asura, should come to support, show reverence, and make offerings, just like they would at a stupa dedicated to the Buddha. If someone can correctly understand and uphold this sutra, that person will attain supreme enlightenment and realize their true nature, becoming a Buddha. Therefore, the place where this sutra is found, is the dwelling of the Buddha, and should be revered and offered to. Such a disciple of the Buddha is also worthy of our respect."

13. Practicing in the Right Way

Subhuti asked the Buddha, "World-Honored One, what name should we give to this sutra? How should we practice according to the teachings of this sutra?"

The Buddha said, "Let this scripture be named 'The Diamond Sutra of Prajnaparamita,' signifying that the wisdom of emptiness is as sharp as a diamond, indestructible by all things, capable of cutting through all phenomena, severing all afflictions, and leading us from the suffering of this shore to the liberation of the other shore. You should practice in accordance with the true meaning of the scripture's name. Why do I say this? Subhuti, the Prajnaparamita that the Buddha is teaching is about the wisdom of emptiness. However, the Prajnaparamita teaching, this Dharma, arises dependent on conditions and lacks an inherent characteristic. It is not inherently existing with no birth and no death; its nature is emptiness. For the convenience of communication, the Buddha used the term "Prajnaparamita" to convey to us the wisdom of liberation through realizing emptiness. Subhuti, do you think the Buddha ever taught a doctrine whose essence is not emptiness? "

"No, Buddha."

"Subhuti, do you think adding together all the dust particles in three thousand great thousandfold worlds would result in a large number?"

Subhuti replied, "Buddha, it would be an extremely vast number."

"Subhuti, these dust particles arise dependent on conditions and lack an inherent characteristic. They are not inherently existing with no birth and no death; their nature is emptiness. However, for the convenience of communication, we use the term 'dust particles' to represent the discussed material. Three thousand great thousandfold worlds are also dependent arising and lack an inherent characteristic. They are not inherently existing with no birth and no death; their nature is also emptiness. However, from a relative perspective, for the sake of linguistic communication, 'three thousand great thousandfold worlds' is used to describe a spatial extent."

"Subhuti, do you think one can recognize Buddhahood through the thirty-two physical characteristics a person may possess?"

"Buddha, it is not possible. The reason is that the thirty-two physical characteristics on your body arise dependently, based on conditions, and lack any inherent, unchanging characteristics. They are not inherently existing; they are not without birth and death; their nature is emptiness. The transient thirty-two physical characteristics on your body cannot be equated with the formless Buddha-nature."

"Subhuti, if there is a virtuous person, regardless of gender, who practice generosity by offering with as many bodies and lifetimes as the grains of sand in the Ganges River; and another person, as long as they can correctly understand and adhere to the teachings of this scripture or even just its four-line verses, and can accurately explain it to others from the perspective of emptiness, the formless merits acquired by such an individual far surpass the merits obtained by those who engage in acts of generosity with their bodies and lives.

14. Non-Abiding in Characteristics

"After hearing the Buddha's teachings on the reality of emptiness, Subhuti was deeply moved, and tears welled up in his eyes. He said to the Buddha, 'Buddha, although I have attained Arhatship, I have never heard such profound and subtle wisdom before. Buddha, if someone, after listening to this scripture, can clearly perceive the emptiness of the phenomena world and life, then we can

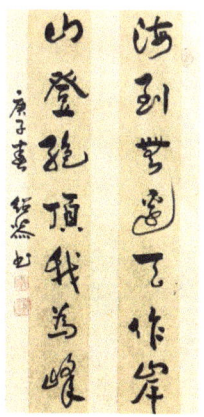

conclude that this person has attained the most supreme and rare formless merits. Buddha, the reality of the phenomena world and life is emptiness, beyond grasping. For the purpose of communication, you have temporarily used the term 'reality,' but in truth, it is formless."

"Buddha, I can now hear this scripture and correctly understand and uphold its true meaning, which is not difficult for me. However, five hundred years from now, if someone encounters this scripture and can correctly understand and uphold its true meaning, we should know that such a person is truly exceptional and remarkable!"

"Why is this so? Because this person has already realized that the characteristics of self, person, sentient being, and life span of sentient being are not inherently existing, are not without birth and death as ultimate truths. This person has comprehended that the nature of self, person, sentient being, and life span of sentient being is emptiness. Therefore, this person does not cling to the characteristics of self, person, sentient being, and life span of sentient being. As long as one sees emptiness and does not cling to any characteristic, this person can be called a Buddha."

The Buddha said to Subhuti, "Yes, yes. If someone, after hearing the profound and subtle teachings on the emptiness in this scripture, can feel neither shocked, nor fearful, nor frightened, then that person is indeed very rare. Why is this so, Subhuti? It is because this person has realized the first paramita that I have spoken of, which is the wisdom of emptiness, formlessness, and liberation. The first paramita does not possess an inherent characteristic that is without birth and death, its essence is also emptiness. For the purpose of communication, the Buddha has used the term 'first paramita.' Subhuti, in the same way, the paramita of tolerance does not possess an inherent characteristic that is without birth and death, its essence is also emptiness. For the purpose of communication, the Buddha has used the term paramita of tolerance."

"Subhuti, in my past lives, when my body was being dismembered by King Kalinga, I did not grasp onto the characteristics of self, person, sentient being, and life span of sentient being. If, at that time, I had clung to any of these characteristics, I would have surely developed feelings of hatred. However, at that moment, I had no feelings of hatred."

"Subhuti, in my past lives, I practiced tolerance for five hundred lifetimes, ultimately achieving the perfection of tolerance. I was able to have no attachment to the characteristics of self, person, sentient being, and life span of sentient being. Therefore, I say, Subhuti, Bodhisattvas should aspire to attain the highest, perfect enlightenment, the great aspiration to Buddhahood, on the basis of not clinging to any characteristic and being far from all characteristics. Bodhisattvas should not let their minds dwell on attachment to form; they should not let their minds dwell on attachment to sound, smell, taste, touch, or thought. Bodhisattvas should let their minds dwell on not attaching to any characteristic. If a Bodhisattva's mind attaches to any characteristic, then that Bodhisattva will have afflictions, and the mind will not correctly give rise to thoughts, nor will it be able to abide correctly."

"So, the Buddha often said, 'For the benefit of all beings, a Bodhisattva should not practice offering with attachment to form, sound, smell, taste, touch, or thought. The Buddha says that the nature of all characteristics is emptiness; the nature of all beings is also emptiness. Subhuti, the Buddha speaks the truth, and what the Buddha says is in accordance with the doctrine of emptiness. The Buddha absolutely does not deceive beings, and what the Buddha says is consistent throughout. Subhuti, the Dharma realized by the Buddha is formless, it is emptiness, and yet when all conditions are fulfilled, it can produce infinite wonderful functions. If a Bodhisattva's mind is attached to the act of giving by the Bodhisattva themselves, it is like a person entering a dark place where nothing can be seen, and this Bodhisattva cannot see the true nature of things, cannot see emptiness. If a Bodhisattva's mind is unattached to the act of giving by the Bodhisattva themselves, it is like a person with normal vision who can see everything in the sunlight. This Bodhisattva can see the true nature of things, and can see emptiness."

"Subhuti, in the future, a virtuous person, whether male or

female, who can frequently recite, correctly understand and uphold the true meaning of this scripture, will gradually have their wisdom awakened. The all-knowing and all-seeing Buddha will be fully aware of this. Such a person will achieve immeasurable and boundless merits."

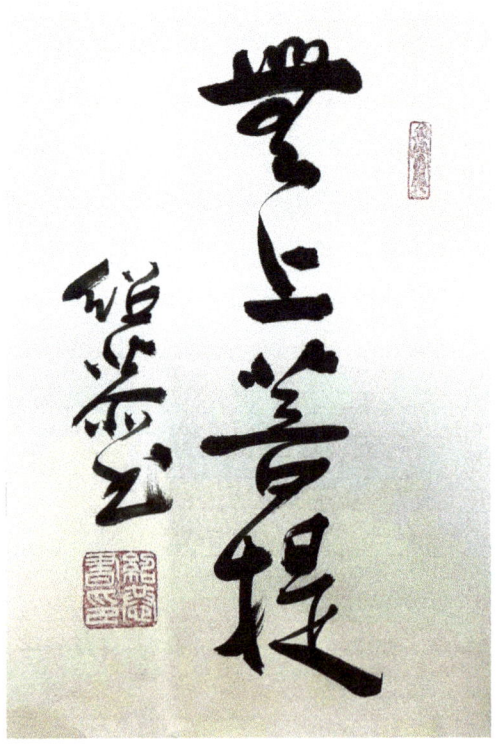

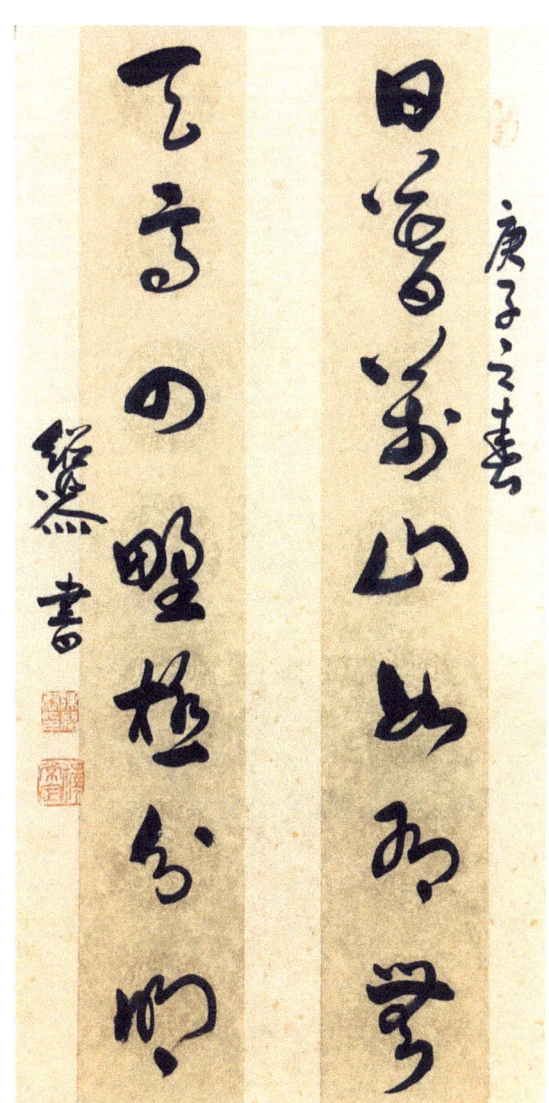

日暮蒼山遠

天寒白屋貧

故說般若波羅蜜多咒是大神咒是大明咒是無上咒是無等等咒能除一切苦真實不虛故說般若波羅蜜多咒

15. The Merits of Correctly Understanding and Upholding the Teaching of Emptiness in the Diamond Sutra

"Subhuti, if a virtuous man or woman practices generosity by offering their own bodies as many times as the number of sand grains in the Ganges River, in the early morning, midday, and afternoon, respectively, for as long as immeasurable trillions of trillions of years; However, if another person, upon hearing this Diamond Sutra, can awaken to the wisdom of emptiness, establish correct faith, and practice according to the teachings of the Buddha, then the merit accumulated by this person, though intangible, far surpasses the merit of the former. If this person not only comprehends and upholds the true meaning of this sutra but also regularly writes, recites, or explains it to others, the merit they accrue will be even greater."

"Subhuti, in summary, the Buddha expounded this sutra for the bodhisattvas who practice Mahayana Buddhism and for those who cultivate the highest wisdom to see the true nature of reality. Therefore, this sutra possesses inconceivable, immeasurable, and boundless merits. If there are individuals who can correctly understand, uphold, recite, and consistently explain this sutra to others, the Buddha will fully acknowledge them. They will attain immeasurable, indescribable, infinite, and inconceivable merit. They are the ones who will attain perfect, unsurpassable enlightenment and assist others in achieving Buddhahood."

"Why is that, Subhuti? Those who are solely interested in self-liberation tend to be attached to the characteristics of a self, a person, a sentient being, or the lifespan of a sentient being. They will not comprehend the profound meaning of this sutra, they will not be inclined to learn, understand, recite, or correctly explain this sutra to others. Therefore, Subhuti, regardless of where it is found, as long as this Diamond Sutra exists, all beings in the world, including heavenly beings, humans, and asuras, should offer their respect and homage with flowers and incense. They should regard this place as a sacred Buddhist temple and devoutly circumambulate it in reverence."

16. Eliminating Karmic Obstacles Accumulated Over Countless Eons

"Furthermore, Subhuti, if a virtuous man or woman, who can correctly understand, uphold, recite, and consistently explain this sutra to others, faces disdain and slander from others, in such a case, you should understand that this is a result of their past negative karma. Without the opportunity to understand, practice, uphold, and recite this sutra, they would have been reborn in the three painful lower realms in their future lives. However, because they can correctly understand and uphold the Diamond Sutra, this portion of their past negative karma is prematurely manifested, leading to its elimination and extinguishment through the disdain and slander of others. They will attain anuttara-samyak-sambodhi—the Buddhahood in the future."

"Subhuti, a very long time ago, in my previous life when Dipankara was the Buddha of the world, I made offerings to Buddhas, totaling 804 trillions of countless Buddhas without missing a single one. However, If someone in the Buddhist time of the Degenerate Age of Dharma can truly understand, practice, uphold, and recite this sutra, the merit they gain surpasses the merit of my offerings to the Buddhas. The merit they will attain is so vast that it cannot be quantified by numbers, nor can it be metaphorically described accurately. The merit I obtained from making offerings to the countless Buddhas during the countless periods of time, is less than one hundredth of merit they will attain, cannot equal to one trillionth of merit they will attain."

"Subhuti, you should understand that the teachings of the Diamond Sutra are incredibly profound, and the resulting karmic outcomes are beyond imagination. If a virtuous man or woman can correctly understand, practice, uphold, and recite this sutra during the Buddhist time of the Degenerate Age of Dharma, the merit they will attain is immeasurable and infinite. If I were to accurately describe all these merits, it might lead some people in the Degenerate Age of Dharma to completely disbelieve, to the point of causing them severe mental distress and madness."

17. I Am Emptiness

Subhuti then asked the Buddha, "O Rare World-Honored One, when virtuous men or women develop the Supreme Perfect Enlightenment, the Buddha's mind of anuttara-samyak-sambodhi, how should they abide and tame their grasping minds."

The Buddha replied to Subhuti, saying, "Virtuous men and women who cultivate the mind of Supreme Perfect Enlightenment, the Buddha's mind of anuttara-samyak-sambodhi, should hold this aspiration: 'I will liberate all sentient beings, enabling them to be free from suffering and attain happiness.' However, I understand that sentient beings are comprised of the five aggregates, constituted by the interplay of these aggregates due to specific conditions. Their essence is emptiness. Therefore, from the ultimate perspective, there is no sentient being that inherently exists as truly born or truly extinguished. Given that sentient beings do not truly exist, the notion of needing to save them also does not truly exist. We simply use the term 'sentient beings' for the sake of communication. How should we understand this? If a Bodhisattva perceives sentient beings as inherently real, then that Bodhisattva becomes attached to concepts of a self, a person, a sentient being, or the lifespan of a sentient being, and such a Bodhisattva is not a genuine Bodhisattva."

"Why is this, Subhuti? The nature of the Dharma is emptiness, even though the Dharma can guide us in cultivating the Buddha's mind of anuttara-samyak-sambodhi on a relative level. Therefore, there is no truly, unconditionally, independently existing Dharma. Subhuti, what is your perspective on this matter? When, in a past life, I learned from Buddha Dipankara, did I acquire a Dharma that truly exists at the ultimate level, enabling me to attain the Buddha's mind of anuttara-samyak-sambodhi?"

Subhuti replied to the Buddha, "No, Rare World-Honored One, I don't believe so. Based on my understanding of the Buddha's teachings, when Buddha Dipankara was your teacher, you did not learn a Dharma called anuttara-samyak-sambodhi that truly exists at the ultimate level."

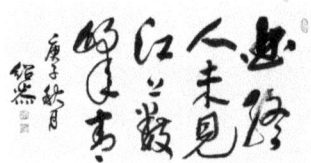

The Buddha replied, "Subhuti, you have spoken well. The essence of Supreme Perfect Enlightenment, the Dharma of anuttara-samyak-sambodhi, is emptiness. In the ultimate level, there is no truly existent dharma. Even though dharma could lead us to attain the Buddha's mind of anuttara-samyak-sambodhi in the relative level. For the sake of communication, we conventionally call it the Dharma of anuttara-samyak-sambodhi. If, at that time, I had believed that dharma was truly, unconditionally existent in the ultimate level, which would lead us to attain the Buddha's mind of anuttara-samyak-sambodhi, then Buddha Dipankara would not have prophesied: 'In the future, you will attain Buddhahood and will be named Buddha Sakyamuni.' Who is the Buddha, the Tathagata? The Tathagata, in reality, refers to the one who comprehends that everything is just as it is, unchanging, and that is emptiness. Subhuti, the essence of all phenomena is emptiness. Therefore, the essence of the Dharma of anuttara-samyak-sambodhi is characterized by emptiness."

"However, on a relative level, the dharma of anuttara-samyak-sambodhi functions for its purpose and led the Buddha to attain the Buddha's mind of anuttara-samyak-sambodhi. Therefore, we say that the dharma of anuttara-samyak-sambodhi neither truly exists on the ultimate level nor is it non-existent on the relative level. When all the necessary conditions are present, infinite wonders can be created from this emptiness. This is what we mean when we say that everything is created by the mind of consciousness, and all phenomena are inseparable from their Buddha's nature. We say that all phenomena are Buddhadharma. Subhuti, when we communicate, we use all phenomena to convey meaning, but in reality, there is no inherently existing entity called "all phenomena" that is beyond birth and death. This remains true: the essence of all phenomena is emptiness, and they do not possess true inherent existence. Subhuti, for instance, what do you think if a person's body is huge, does this constitute a truly existent huge body?"

Subhuti responded, "Buddha, when you speak of a person's

body being tall and large, it is for the sake of communication. In reality, a person's body arises from conditions and causes and is not inherently, permanently, , or unconditionally existent. Its true nature is emptiness, and it is not a truly existing entity; its essence is emptiness. Furthermore, even if this body is large, it still has dimensions. What is truly vast is the Buddha's Dharma body, the dharmakaya, which is formless and immeasurable by dimensions."

"A Bodhisattva understands the principle that the nature of phenomena is emptiness. If a Bodhisattva perceives the sentient beings they liberate as inherently born or truly existent, then that Bodhisattva has not grasped the essence of emptiness and cannot be considered a genuine Bodhisattva. Therefore, the Buddha teaches that in all phenomena, there is fundamentally no truly existing self, person, sentient being, or life span of sentient being. These aspects simply do not exist."

"Furthermore, if a Bodhisattva cannot perceive emptiness and believes that a Buddha land possesses an inherently existing form, then such a Bodhisattva is not truly a Bodhisattva. Why is this the case? A genuine Buddha land is our Buddha's nature. When, while observing all phenomena, one comprehends the present emptiness within these phenomena, allowing the mind to remain without attachment, that is what truly adorns a Buddha land."

"Subhuti, a true Bodhisattva can profoundly realize the principle that both the self and all phenomena are characterized by emptiness."

18. Same Buddha's Nature
"Subhuti, what do you think? Does the Buddha have flesh eyes?"

"Yes, the Rare World-Honored One, the Buddha has flesh eyes."

The Buddha asked, "Subhuti, do you think the Buddha possesses the divine eye endowed with supernatural powers?"

Subhuti replied, "Yes, the Rare World-Honored One, the Buddha has the divine eye endowed with supernatural powers."

The Buddha asked, "Subhuti, do you think the Buddha has the wisdom eye that can see the essential emptiness of all phenomena?"

Subhuti replied, "Yes, the Rare World-Honored One, the Buddha has the wisdom eye."

The Buddha asked, "Subhuti, do you think the Buddha has the Dharma eye that can see the empty nature of all phenomena without attachment to illusionary forms and characteristics created by all phenomena?"

Subhuti replied, "Yes, the Rare World-Honored One, the Buddha has the Dharma eye."

The Buddha asked, "Subhuti, do you think the Buddha has the Buddha eye that can see the Buddha's nature?"

Subhuti replied, "Yes, the Rare World-Honored One, the Buddha has the Buddha eye."

The Buddha asked, "Subhuti, do you think there are many grains of sand in the Ganges River?" Subhuti replied, "Yes, Buddha, there are many grains of sand in the Ganges."

The Buddha asked, "Subhuti, if each grain of sand in the Ganges were to become a Ganges River, and you added up the number of sand grains in each of those Ganges Rivers. Let's say we designate the total number of sand grains as 'x.' If there were x number of Buddha worlds, do you think that would be considered many?"

Subhuti replied, "Buddha, it would be too numerous to count."

The Buddha said, "In all these many Buddha worlds, I know the thoughts and intentions of all sentient beings. Why is this? It is because the thoughts of all sentient beings arise from the Buddha-nature when the conditions and causes come together, and this Buddha-nature pervades everything. Therefore, in all these countless Buddha worlds, I fully comprehend the thoughts and intentions of all sentient beings. Thoughts do not possess an inherent essence. At the moment of their arising, thoughts set in motion the process of their birth and cessation, revealing the empty nature of thoughts. Similarly, when we speak of past thoughts, present thoughts, and future thoughts, they are all just thoughts and not inherently existing entities. Their essence is emptiness."

19. The Greatest Merit of Non-Abiding Generosity

"Subhuti, if someone were to give away treasures enough to fill three thousand great thousandfold worlds, what do you think? Would the merit acquired by that person be tremendous?"

"Buddha, the merit gained by that person would be immeasurable."

"Subhuti, the essence of merit is emptiness. However, for the convenience of communication, we speak of the merit gained as abundant. If a Bodhisattva understands that merit arises due to the coming together of causes and conditions, comprehends the emptiness nature of merit, and does not cling to the illusory characteristics of its arising and ceasing, then the merit obtained by that Bodhisattva is the greatest."

20. Not Clinging to Any Characteristic While Walking the Bodhisattva Path

"Subhuti, do you think the Buddha-nature, which is neither born nor extinguished, is the same as the perfected body of a Buddha's physical manifestation?"

"Buddha, absolutely not. Why do I say this? The perfected body (**Nirmāṇakāya**) of a Buddha's physical manifestation is composed of the four elements: earth, water, fire, and air. It is conditioned, subject to birth and cessation; it is not the Buddha-nature itself. The Buddha-nature is unborn and undying, it is formless, and it is the true body of the Buddha. For the sake of communication, the Buddha uses the term 'perfectly fulfilled Nirmāṇakāya' as an expression."

"Subhuti, what do you think? Can the Buddha-nature be measured and distinguished by the thirty-two physical characteristics and eighty auspicious signs of the Buddha?"

"Buddha, absolutely cannot use the thirty-two physical characteristics and eighty auspicious signs possessed by the Nirmāṇakāya Buddha as a standard to measure and distinguish the authenticity of Buddha-nature. Why is this? Because the Buddha-nature is formless, while the thirty-two physical characteristics and eighty auspicious signs of the Nirmāṇakāya Buddha arise dependently, with conditions, and are subject to birth and cessation. Thus, the thirty-two physical characteristics and eighty auspicious signs are not the Buddha-nature itself. However, for the sake of communication, they are provisionally used to describe the Nirmāṇakāya Buddha."

21. The Things Expressed by Language Are Not Truly Existing

"Subhuti, absolutely do not hold onto the thought that the teachings I present are truly existent and neither born nor extinguished. Why do I say this? If someone claims that the teachings spoken by the Buddha are truly existent and neither born nor extinguished, then this person has fundamentally failed to understand the true meaning and purpose of my teachings. Subhuti, all phenomena are emptiness, and the teachings I expound arise from the coming together of causes and conditions; their essence is emptiness. There is no such thing as a teaching that is neither born nor extinguished, or truly existent. However, for the sake of facilitating communication, I use the term 'teaching' to convey the essence of what is taught."

At this moment, the wise Subhuti asked the Buddha, "Buddha, in the future, when sentient beings hear the teachings you are presenting now about the doctrine of emptiness, will they be able to believe and comprehend the principles of emptiness that you are expounding?"

The Buddha replied, "Subhuti, from the Buddha's ultimate perspective, there are no beings that are truly existent and neither born nor extinguished. Sentient beings arise from causes and conditions, and therefore, they will inevitably experience birth and cessation, which does not align with the Buddhist definition of absolute existence. However, in the relative world of ordinary individuals, there are relatively existent sentient beings. For the purpose of communication, we use the term 'sentient beings' to describe this relative existence."

22. The Essence of the Supreme and Perfect Enlightenment Dharma Is Emptiness

Subhuti said to the Buddha, "Buddha, you have attained what is called the Supreme and Perfect Enlightenment, the Anuttara-Samyak-Sambodhi. Although it is said this way, Buddha has not obtained something that is truly existent and neither born nor extinguished, called the Supreme and Perfect Enlightenment (Anuttara-Samyak-Sambodhi)."

The Buddha replied, "Subhuti, you are correct. The Buddha has indeed attained the Supreme and Perfect Enlightenment, the Anuttara-Samyak-Sambodhi, and thereby knows all phenomena. However, the Buddha has not attained something that is truly existent, and neither born nor extinguished, called the Supreme and Perfect Enlightenment. The Dharma of Anuttara-Samyak-Sambodhi arises from the coming together of causes and conditions; its essence is emptiness, devoid of any truly existent and neither born nor extinguished characteristics. Nevertheless, for the purpose of communication, we use the term 'Anuttara-Samyak-Sambodhi' to describe this Dharma that enables sentient beings to attain Boddhahood."

23. Cultivating All Virtuous Qualities with an Unattached Pure Mind

"Furthermore, Subhuti, all phenomena arise from causes and conditions, and none of them possess inherently existing and neither born nor extinguished characteristics. Because all phenomena are characterized by emptiness, when viewed from the perspective of emptiness, all phenomena are equal, with no distinctions of higher or lower. If a practitioner can engage in the practice of all virtuous qualities based on the understanding that the characteristics of self, person, sentient being, or the lifespan of sentient being are emptiness, and if they can engage in these practices without attachment to self, person, sentient being, or the lifespan of sentient being, then that practitioner will attain the Supreme and Perfect Enlightenment, the unsurpassed, complete awakening."

"Subhuti, virtuous qualities also arise from causes and conditions, and none of them possess inherently existing and neither born nor extinguished characteristics. Their essence is characterized by emptiness. However, for the purpose of communication, the term 'virtuous qualities' is used to describe this teaching."

24. The Merits of Practice with Characteristics and Without Characteristics Are Incomparable

"Subhuti, if someone were to give away all the seven jewels, filling up all the Mount Sumerus in the three-thousandfold universe, and if another person could understand, practice, uphold, recite, and explain to others this Diamond Sutra, or even only four-line verses, the merit attained by the latter would far exceed that of the former. The merit attained by the former would be less than one hundredth, one thousandth, or one millionth of that of the latter; the difference is so immense that it cannot be adequately expressed even through mathematical calculation."

25. Sentient Beings Do Not Truly Exist; Their Essence Is Emptiness

"Subhuti, you must never think that the beings whom the Buddha liberates are truly existent. Beings do not possess any inherent characteristic; their essence is emptiness. If the Buddha were to perceive beings as truly existent, it would imply attachment to self, person, sentient being, or the lifespan of sentient being. Similarly, Subhuti, when the Buddha speaks of 'self,' there is no 'self' with inherent characteristic; its essence is emptiness. Unfortunately, ordinary people mistakenly believe that this physical body's 'self' is truly existent. Ordinary people do not possess any inherent characteristic; their essence is also emptiness. For the sake of communication, we use the term 'ordinary people' to convey the meaning."

26. Formless Dharma Body (*dharmakāya*)

"Subhuti, do you believe that by seeing a Buddha here (Nirmāṇakāya or Manifestation body) with the magnificent thirty-two physical characteristics, you have truly seen the real Buddha?"

Subhuti replied, "Yes, seeing a Buddha with thirty-two physical characteristics is indeed seeing the real Buddha."

"Subhuti, if we use the thirty-two physical characteristics as the standard, even a Wheel-Turning Sacred King possesses them. Does that mean a Wheel-Turning Sacred King who rules over the four great continents of one universe, is also the real Buddha?"

Subhuti immediately said to the Buddha, "Buddha, I now understand that the true Buddha is the Buddha-nature, the pure Buddha's mind, which is formless. Therefore, one cannot use the thirty-two physical characteristics as a criterion to distinguish the true Buddha."

Upon hearing this, the Buddha recited four line verses:
"If someone thinks that the physical form they see is the real Buddha—Buddha nature, if someone thinks that through vocal supplication, they can invoke the presence of the true Buddha,—Buddha nature, These individuals, by focusing on external appearances, seek the formless Buddha nature, which is our own pure nature. Such an approach is misguided, and they can never truly perceive the authentic Buddha, which means they cannot recognize

our own inherent purity-Buddha's nature."

27. Non-Attachment to the Empty Nature of Phenomena

"Subhuti, if you think this way: since the true Buddha is the Buddha-nature, and Buddha-nature is formless, then the manifested Buddha does not necessarily need to possess the thirty-two characteristics to attain Anuttara-samyak-sambodhi, the unsurpassed, perfect awakening. Subhuti, you must never hold such a notion that denies the interdependent origination of causes and conditions. Why is that? As we cultivate the mind to attain Buddhahood, we should neither attach the emptiness of phenomena nor negate the relative existence of causes and conditions."

28. Non-Attachment to Attributes

"Subhuti, imagine there are two Bodhisattvas. One practices generosity and fills space in as many worlds as there are grains of sand in the Ganges with seven treasures. The other Bodhisattva has attained the profound wisdom of non-arising, realizing the emptiness and selflessness of all phenomena. The merit gained by the latter Bodhisattva surpasses that of the former. Subhuti, why is this so? It's because the latter Bodhisattva has no attachment to any merit."

Subhuti asked the Buddha, "What is the reason that leads these bodhisattvas to not cling to the attributes of merit?"

"Subhuti, these bodhisattvas understand that the merit they attain is generated by the coming together of causes and conditions. There is no inherently existing and neither birth nor extinguished characteristics in merits; its essence is emptiness. Since these bodhisattvas understand that the essence of merit is emptiness, they do not develop attachment to merit, which is not inherently existent."

29. It Neither Comes from Outside, Nor Does It Depart From Here; It Has Always Been There; This Is Called the Tathāgata

"Subhuti, if someone, upon seeing the coming, going, sitting, and lying down of a manifested Buddha, thinks that the true Buddha must also possess characteristics of coming, going, sitting, and lying down, and regards these as real existences, then this person's thinking is entirely mistaken. Why is this said so? 'Tathagata' refers to the pure intrinsic nature of the Buddha, which is the Buddha-nature. The characteristic of Buddha-nature is formless. Buddha-nature has always been there, without any coming or going involved."

30. Emptiness Is Formless

"Subhuti, if we were to crush a three-thousandfold world into tiny specks of dust, would there be many specks of dust?"

Subhuti replied, "Buddha, there would be an immense number of specks of dust. However, none of these specks of dust possesses an inherent characteristic or an unchanging form. They are generated by the coming together of causes and conditions and, therefore, do not exist as true entities in the Buddhist ultimate perspective. Their essence is emptiness. We use the term 'specks of dust' for the sake of communication. Similarly, a three-thousandfold world does not possess an inherent characteristic or an unchanging form. It, too, is generated by the coming together of causes and conditions and does not exist as a true entity in the Buddhist ultimate perspective. Its essence is emptiness. We use the term three-thousandfold world for the sake of communication."

"A three-thousandfold world is generated by the coming together of causes and conditions, and its essence is emptiness. However, emptiness itself does not possess an inherent characteristic or a fixed form , so it is said to be formless. For the purpose of communication, the term 'the appearance of compound oneness' is used to represent the other aspect of dependent origination, which is emptiness. Dependent origination and emptiness are two aspects that coexist in all phenomena."

"Subhuti, emptiness can only be personally experienced, and one can only sense their own warmth and coldness. Language and words cannot truly express the nature of emptiness itself. However, worldly individuals mistakenly believe that emptiness has an inherent characteristic or fixed form and become attached to this illusory, non-existent form."

31. The Nature of Knowledge and Perception Is Emptiness

"Subhuti, if someone says, 'The Buddha always mentions the view of self, person, sentient being, and life span of sentient being, then the view of self, person, sentient being, and life span of sentient being, must definitely exist in the authentic sense in Buddhism. Subhuti, do you think this person truly grasps the true significance of what I am conveying?"

"Buddha, this person fundamentally does not understand the true meaning that you, the Buddha, intend to convey. I say this because you, the Buddha, use terms like the view of self, person, sentient being, and life span of sentient being for the purpose of communication. In reality, the view of self, person, sentient being, and life span of sentient being, is also generated by the coming together of causes and conditions and have emptiness as their essence."

"Subhuti, similarly, those who cultivate the mind to attain Anuttara-samyak-sambodhi, the unsurpassed, perfect awakening, should view all phenomena from the perspective of the fundamental emptiness of all things and practice all virtuous dharmas. They should neither get attached to existence nor get attached to emptiness. Subhuti, when the Buddha speaks of the emptiness, it is also for the purpose of communication, using the term emptiness. You must never mistakenly think that the emptiness has an unchanging, truly existent characteristic or form . If you think this way, it would be a grave mistake."

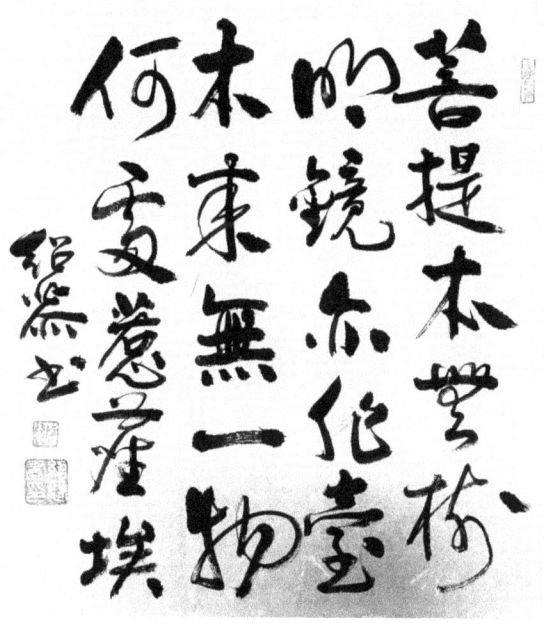

32. Manifested Buddhas Are Not the True Bodies of Buddhas

"Subhuti, if someone were to fill countless, immeasurable, and boundless worlds with the seven treasures and make offerings with such a vast quantity of treasures, and if there were other men and women who, with a mind to attain Buddhahood and help sentient beings, could correctly understand, uphold, recite, and consistently explain the profound meaning in this scripture to others, or the true essence in the four-line verse within it, the merit gained by the latter would far surpass that of the former who made offerings with the seven treasures. Why is that? It is because the latter can perceive the aspect of emptiness and do not cling to all phenomena."

"All phenomena that arise from the coming together of causes and conditions are subject to birth and cessation; they do not exist as true realities in ultimate level. Their appearance is like a dream, like morning dew, like lightning in the sky—fleeting and momentary. We should view all phenomena with this awareness!"

After the Buddha completed the teaching of this sutra,

Venerable Subhuti, the elder and senior monk, along with all the monks, nuns, male and female lay practitioners, as well as heavenly beings, human beings, and asuras in this world, were filled with joy and gained faith in the Dharma. They all made a vow to diligently understand and practice in accordance with the Buddha's teachings.

即说咒曰 揭谛 揭谛 波罗揭谛 波罗僧揭谛

Dedication Verse

May the merits of reciting the Diamond Sutra,
Adorn the Buddha's Pure Land.
Repay the fourfold kindness above,
Relieve the suffering of the three paths below.

For those who hear and understand,
May they all generate the Bodhi mind.
With this single dedicatory body,
May we be reborn together in the Land of Ultimate Bliss.

About the Author

Pingping Huang was born in China and moved to the United States in the early 1990s. She obtained a BBA in Finance and Investment from the Zicklin School of Business at Baruch College in New York City. After graduation, she began her financial career at a Fortune 500 company on Wall Street. Currently, she serves as the Secretary-General of The International Hua-Yan Buddhist Federation and is also the English Secretary for the American Buddhist Confederation. Pingping began exploring Buddhism in 1991 and took refuge in the Three Jewels (Buddha, Dharma, and Sangha) under the late Venerable Ben Huan, the 44th generation lineage holder of China's Linji Chan School (1907-2012).

Pingping harbors a wish, hoping that every reader of this scripture can immediately grasp its central idea. Therefore, after completing the translation of the "Diamond Sutra" into colloquial English, she decided to further translate it into modern, easily understood vernacular Chinese. As everyone can see, she strives to use the everyday language of ordinary people. The Buddhist Dharma is immeasurably vast, and Pingping is grateful for the opportunity to share her translation with all.

www.ingramcontent.com/pod-product-compliance
Lightning Source LLC
Chambersburg PA
CBHW061253230426
43665CB00026B/2920